期权成交量对KOSPI200股指收益和波动的预测力：基于韩国证券市场

The Predictive Power of Options Volume for the Return and Volatility of KOSPI200 Index: Evidence from Korean Security Markets

康明惠／著

西南财经大学出版社
四川・成都

图书在版编目(CIP)数据

期权成交量对 KOSPI200 股指收益和波动的预测力:基于韩国证券市场/康明惠著.—成都:西南财经大学出版社,2020.7
ISBN 978-7-5504-4445-4

Ⅰ.①期… Ⅱ.①康… Ⅲ.①股票指数期货—期货交易—研究—韩国—英文 Ⅳ.①F833.126.5

中国版本图书馆 CIP 数据核字(2020)第 128804 号

期权成交量对 KOSPI200 股指收益和波动的预测力:基于韩国证券市场
QIQUAN CHENGJIAOLIANG DUI KOSPI200 GUZHI SHOUYI HE BODONG DE YUCELI:
JIYU HANGUO ZHENGQUAN SHICHANG
康明惠 著

总 策 划:李玉斗
责任编辑:何春梅
封面设计:墨创文化
责任印制:朱曼丽

出版发行	西南财经大学出版社(四川省成都市光华村街 55 号)
网 址	http://www.bookcj.com
电子邮件	bookcj@foxmail.com
邮政编码	610074
电 话	028-87353785
照 排	四川胜翔数码印务设计有限公司
印 刷	四川新财印务有限公司
成品尺寸	170mm×240mm
印 张	11.25
字 数	201 千字
版 次	2020 年 7 月第 1 版
印 次	2020 年 7 月第 1 次印刷
书 号	ISBN 978-7-5504-4445-4
定 价	68.00 元

前　言

股指的收益和波动直接反映风险溢价，对于投资者预测资产定价以及衍生商品的组合投资策略、风险管理尤为重要，但是目前学界关于分析期权交易量和收益与波动的相关研究并不多。现有的文献大部分通过建立静态单一的方程分别研究股指期货、融资融券、现货市场的信息交易，模型过于简单，无法很好地反映跨市场信息交易的隐蔽性和复杂性。真实金融市场往往处于一个动态变化的复杂系统中，各市场的相关变量往往是互相作用、互为因果的，并且信息交易者为了追求利益最大化，往往不会只在单一市场进行投资，而是会选择通过跨市场操作来实现“利益效应”的放大，因而有必要将这些代表不同市场的信息变量纳入一个系统的模型中进行分析。

目前大部分学者的研究主要集中在金融衍生品市场与现货市场之间的领先—滞后关系上，并没有进一步研究这样的领先—滞后关系究竟是由什么原因导致的。套利交易、信息交易或者其流动性都可能导致跨市场交易的收益和波动的领先和滞后关系，但却很少有学者通过实证研究进一步分析导致跨市场交易的领先—滞后关系的真正原因，大部分的现有研究只是直接假设这种领先—滞后关系是由信息交易导致的。对跨市场间信息交易的影响因素和信息交易者投资偏好的研究不够深入，缺乏从市场微观结构和行为交易的角度来分析影响跨市场信息交易的因素，并且也没有阐明持有不同信息的交易者是如何构建差异化的跨市场投资策略的。

基于以上提到的不足，本书以目前世界期权交易最活跃的韩国KOSPI200股指期权为研究对象，研究股指期权成交量与现货市场收益波动之间的关系，试图从以下几个方面来完善现有的研究：①研究信息交易者在持有重要优势信息时，是否存在韩国期权和现货的跨市场信息交易行为；探讨可能的信息交易对市场的收益、波动和流动性的影响。②揭示在利好、利空的消息背景下，信息交易者的投资偏好和投资策略。③研究具有不同投资目的的信息交易者如何构建动态投资策略。④信息交易明确影响跨市场交易的因素。⑤识别可能存在的跨市场信息交易者。⑥阐明跨市场信息交易的识别机制。

本书的研究与现有研究的差异主要体现在以下几个方面：

首先，考虑到以往利用Black-Sholes或者Put-Call Parity期权定价模型来测定收益波动的研究存在理论上的诸多限制条件的约束，本书利用5分钟的高频数据，将期权成交量和Put-Call比率分为可预测部分和不可预测部分，来预测其是否会对现货KOSPI200股指产生影响，发现在期权市场存在一定的信息交易，期权市场对现货市场波动的影响大于现货市场对期权市场的影响。以往研究大都认为，期权市场与现货市场之间的领先—滞后关系是以信息交易为假设前提的，但很少有研究直接探讨期权市场与现货市场之间的领先—滞后关系产生的根本原因，其实在实际交易中这种关系可能也受投资者对冲策略和流动性的影响，本书试图通过把期权交易量与宏观信息变量等比率联系在一起，探索信息交易是否是导致这种领先—滞后关系的根本原因。实证结果表明期权成交量对 KOPSI200 股指收益和波动的预测力与信息交易有一定的关联性。

其次，本书将投资者分为个人投资者、机构投资者和外国投资者，试图分析不同投资者在韩国股指期权和现货市场上所扮演的角色。与以往的研究对象不同，韩国股指期权市场主要以个人投资者为主，相对于个股而言，股指期权更容易受到整体市场、宏观经济等因素的影响，而机构投资者和外国投资者更具有宏观信息优势和跨国投资分析技术，以及相较于个人投资者较少受到非理性偏差的影响。因此这种不均衡的投资者结构会给机构或者外国投资者提供更多的短期获利机会，这样的数据特征也可以很好地用来审视机构投资者在价格发现中所发挥的作用。韩国证券市场目前还存在对于卖空的限制，这些严格的限制会驱使持有负面消息的信息交易者更倾向于在期权等衍生品市场进行交易，考虑到目前韩国市场相较于美国等发达国家的证券市场而言，仍缺乏对内部交易者的监管和市场有效性，因此韩国证券市场的这些特点给我们分析跨市场信息交易、期权市场与现货市场之间的领先—滞后关系以及在跨市场交易中机构投资者所起到的作用提供了坚实基础。实证结果显示，外国机构投资者的期权成交量对 KOSPI200 指数收益和波动有显著的预测效应，而个人和国内机构投资者的期权成交量对 KOSPI200 指数收益的波动没有显著影响。

最后，考虑到不同价值的期权对信息交易者选择投资策略会有不同的影响，因此有必要分析不同价值的期权成交量对于 KOPSI200 股指收益和波动是否具有不同的预测力，以及信息交易者在构建投资策略时更倾向于选择哪种类型的期权。本书的研究表明，两平期权对 KOSPI200 股指的收益和波动具有最好的预测力，其次是深度虚值期权和虚值期权。

综上所述，本书的研究具有重要的理论意义和实践意义。从理论研究来看，本书的研究不仅有助于深化和丰富跨市场交易领域的价格发现和波动预测研究，还可以有效完善股指期权市场的交易机制，为健全跨市场金融监管提供理论依据和方案。从业界实践来看，本书的研究不仅可以用于分析在信息不对称的情境下不同类型的投资者构建的投资策略，还可以为投资业界的实践优化服务设计提供新的决策参考。

Contents

1 Introduction

1.1 Research Background

The astonishing growth in the derivative market has been witnessed in recent years. Accompanying the impressive growth in size and variety, the role of derivatives as a vehicle for the trading of informed investors has attract many researchers' attention. In particular, options trading gradually plays an increasingly vital role when informed investors build their investment strategies, considering some advantages of options such as the higher leverage, lower transaction cost. Meanwhile, options trading also can be utilized to hedge downside risk of underlying assets and avoid some restriction of short sales. Therefore, in view of theoretical concern, despite options trading should convey no additional information on the underlying assets, in practice, informed traders prefer to choose options as their useful instruments instead of equities to achieve goals of the investment.

While the existing literature has actively focused on the informational role of the options and stock trading volume in predicting the future stock price movements (Chan, Chung & Fong, 2002; Easley, O'Hara & Srinivas, 1998), there is little work to focus on the relation between options volume and volatility of underlying asset. Furthermore, the evidence regarding the information content of the options volume for the volatility of spot index is limited and inclusive. In addition, most of the existing related studies focus on the informed trading in developed country security markets, little works have been done on the information content of options volume for the volatility of underlying asset in the emerging market. This research intends to fill this void by examining the predictive power of options volume for the volatility of KOSPI200 index.

KOSPI200 index options market is substantially different from the S&P500 index options market. Trading in the options market is dominated by individual investors rather than institutional investors. In addition, call options are traded more than put options. Meanwhile, the KOSPI200 index options are the most actively traded index options in the world, thus the market is extremely liquid. The trading volume of the KOSPI200 index options is larger than the sum of the trading volume of S&P100 index options and S&P500 index options. Although there is still tight short-sale constraints and daily price change limit in Korean equity market, the options market in Korea has no short-sale constraints and daily price change limit. These stringent trading regulations in the equity market are expected to steer informed trading from the equity market to the options market. In addition, because an emerging market is less efficient than a mature market, there are less insider trading regulations. Hence, all else equal, trading in an emerging market provides more profitable opportunities for informed traders. These favorable conditions provide solid and robust foundation for analyzing the information content of options volume for the volatility of KOSPI200 index.

1.2 Research Objective

This study is guided by four primary motives. First, this research attempts to investigate the predictive power of options volume for the volatility of KOSPI200 index, by analyzing the dynamic relation between the options volume and the volatility of KOSPI200 index. In this study, in view of the asymmetry in the return series, the volatility of KOSPI200 is estimated by EGARCH (Exponential Generalized Autoregressive Conditional Heteroskedasticity) model. Following the approach of Bessembinder & Segun (1992), options volume and put-call ratio in this study are partitioned into expected component and unexpected component according to the methodology of ARIMA(10,0,10). Expected component stands for public information based on the movement of the historical data, which is usually used to measure the behavior of uninformed trader. Unexpected component represents private information that informed traders acquire correspondingly, which is used to capture the movement of informed trader. In order to investigate the existence of informed trading in Korean Security markets, the volatility of KOSPI200 index is linked with the unexpected options volumes. By using Vector Auto-regression (VAR) equation model to capture the volume-volatility relations, this study finds strong and unambiguous evidence on the predictive power of option volumes for the volatility of KOSPI200.

Second, as a part of further analysis to understand the pattern of informed trading in the option market, this study also attempts to answer the question of whether a certain type of investors has information advantages over other types of investors. Although there is some consensus in the literature that institutional investors have better information access or superior trading ability than individual investors, empirical evidence on whether foreign or domestic investors are more informed is mixed. Moreover, studies on the informational role of institutional investors and foreign investors usually focus on stock markets. Little is known about this issue in the index options market. As to whether foreign or domestic investors have better access to information, index options market may have different implications compared to stock markets. The data for this study comes from the Korean index market and options market. The Korean Stock Exchange was one of the major exchanges in the emerging markets, considering its market capitalization and trading volume. As argued by Richard (2005), although it is very unlikely that anyone might possess private information about the market index in a fairly large equity market, such as the U.S. market, foreign capital inflows in the emerging markets are so large that they can create price pressure. This clearly offers profitable opportunities for those who have access to the information. Since foreign investors play such an important role in the Korea equity market, this motives us to investigate whether the foreign capital flows into the Korean options market also contain information on the future volatility of KOSPI200 index.

One of the unique features of dataset in this study is that each transaction record can be identified for different investor types, which enables to classify the investors into three main investor classifications: domestic institutional investors, foreign investors, individual investors. These features are beneficial to unearth evidence on the informational role of various investor classes, thereby contributing to the literature on the movement of international capital flows in the equity and options markets. The findings of this study suggest that foreign institutional investors have strongest predictive power in the Korean options market, thereby providing evidence that foreign investors do indeed have superior ability to collect and analyze information than other investors.

Third, since different degrees of options′ moneyness have various influences on the choice of informed investors, it is necessary to investigate the information content of different degree of options moneyness for the volatility of KOSPI200 index. In general, this study find ATM options provides the best measure for the volatility of KOSPI200 index, followed by deep OTM options and OTM options.

Finally, most of the previous studies on the information content of options volume regard the assumption that the options volume serves as good proxy for informed trading as premise of their studies. There is scant evidence, however, of any attempt to test this assumption directly. Therefore, inspired by this idea, this research attempts to investigate whether options trading can be due to the behavior of informed investors acting on a direct information source, and determine the type of options in which such investors are more likely to trade. In order to investigate whether the predictive power of the options volume for the volatility of KOSPI200 index is attributed to the informed trading rather than other purposes, such as hedge and liquid, this study relates the unexpected options volume to the macroeconomic news announcement. Because the source of informed trading in the index options market is more likely to be macroeconomic information, rather than firm-specific private information. Moreover, in view of the influence of U. S economy on Korean security markets, six important macroeconomic news announcements each for South Korea and U. S. are selected as exogenous information events in this study. Supposing if the index options trading is not motivated by the information, no information asymmetry should exist among market participants. Options volume should not yield significant reactions to the news announcements. However, if informed trading exists in the index options market, the data should yield significant reactions before the news announcements. This study not only verifies the existence of informed trading, but also finds ATM options are the best vehicle for volatility informed trader.

This research attempts to extend previous studies through systematic and comprehensive examination of the existence of informed trading between spot index market and options market in the emerging market. In particular, the present study supplements existing financial literature in the following major aspects. First, compared with earlier studies, this research uses intraday data instead of daily data to test the existence of informed trading, because intraday data is found to be easier to exploit the behavior of informed trader. In this research, the most up-to-date and comprehensive dataset of 36 985 intraday data is used to test whether the options trading lead the volatility of spot stock market. Second, this study is the first study, according to my knowledge, to directly analyze the relationship between options trading volume and the announcements of macroeconomics news in Korea. In other words, this study seeks to determine whether options volume occurs as a result of the release of news, a claim that has been taken as a premise in the literature but has never been directly proved. Finally, this study also demonstrates that the controversy over mixed results of the prior studies partially attribute to aggregating options data irrespective of investor classification and options moneyness. This study intends to give a rational explanation by analyzing the informational role of various investor classes and options moneyness.

1.3 Organization of the Dissertation

The remainder of this paper is organized as follows. Section 2 provides literature review related to this study. Section 3 provides an introduction to hypotheses and methodology. Section 4 gives a description of dataset in this study. The empirical results are presented in Section 5. Finally, a summary of the results, implication and suggestion for future research are given in section 6.

2 Literature Review

2.1 The Relation Between the Return of Stock Price and Options Trading

Before examining whether the options volume leads the volatility of stock market, it is worthwhile to take a look at the theoretical models related to the relation between stock price and options market. One group of researchers argues that informed investors exploit their private information in options market before in its underlying asset market; thus, the information is disseminated from the option market to the underlying asset market. Manaster & Rendleman (1982) find that options trading leads the trading of the underlying asset. In a similar vein, Chakravarty, Gulen & Mayhew (2004) suggest that options trading contributes to the price discovery of underlying assets. From the view of volume, Pan & Poteshman (2006) argue that the volume of options market leads the movement of underlying asset. Consistent with the preceding notions, Cao & Wei (2010) find distinct evidence that information asymmetry is greater for options trading than for the trading of the underlying asset, implying that agents with private information prefer to use the options market as a efficient venue for trading. This finding is also supported by Easley, O'Hara & Srinivas (1998), who find that options order flows contain information about the future direction of the underlying stock price. They also find that informed traders exploit the leverage of the options market to maximize profitability. While other scholars argue that there is not much evidence that options volume predicts underlying stock prices. Cao, Chen & Griffin (2005) found that during "normal" times, stock volume but not options volume is informative about future stock returns. This finding is supported by Chan, Chung & Fong (2002), who concluded unambiguously that options volume does not lead stock prices.

2.2 The Relation Between the Volatility of Stock Price and Options Trading

The critical determinants of the performance of many asset management tasks such as risk management, derivatives pricing, options trading, hedging, and asset allocation are all centered on the forecasting of future volatility. Modeling and forecasting market volatility has long been an important issue in finance as well as in econometrics. Blair, Poon & Taylor (2001) and Poon & Granger (2003) have summarized that volatility forecasting models can be classified in the following three categories: the historical volatility models (HISVOL), the GARCH family, the options implied standard deviation (ISD) model.

There has been a debate about which is the superior volatility estimation method if any in the sense of forecasting future volatility accuracy. In general, there are two widely used approaches to forecasting the volatility of a financial asset. One of them uses time series techniques (e.g. Andersen & Bollerslev, 1998; Anderson & Vahid, 2007; Hsieh, 1991) and relies on the past behavior of asset prices to infer the future trend. Time series approach (GARCH family), by nature, is backward looking, using past behavior to project future. An alternative approach is to use reported options prices to infer the volatility expectation from options pricing models (implied volatility approach). Implied volatility (IV) is widely interpreted as the market expectation of the underlying stock's return volatility over the remaining life of the option. In practice, one common feature that causes difficulty in the line of implied volatility research is that implied volatility obtained from options on the same underlying with different strikes are different. Furthermore, deep in-the-money and out-of-money options yield higher implied volatilities than near the money options, and such phenomenon is often referred to volatility smile or skew phenomenon.

The approach to estimate the volatility in this paper is motivated by the finding of Ohk & Cheon(2006). They argue that EGARCH method is the best method to be adapted to estimate the future volatility, by comparing the volatility of KOSPI200 index though EGARCH, GARCH and GJS-GARCH method. Furthermore, EGARCH is the optimal approach to estimate the future volatility in term of the asymmetric distribution of the KOSPI200 index, in contrast to the implied volatility method.

In addition to the issue of the optimal multivariate volatility measures, there are other researches focusing on examining the existence of volatility informed trading. Pan & Poteshman (2008) investigate whether informed trading on stock volatility exist in the options market. They use non-market maker net demand for volatility from the trading volume of individual equity options as information variable and find that this demand is informative about the future realized volatility of underlying stocks. Gunther(2004) develops a multimarket sequential trading model with asymmetric information in which directional traders and volatility – traders interact strategically. The major finding is that volatility traders evict directional–traders from the options market. While these results do not confirm that option returns lead spot returns. Following the approach of Pan & Poteshman(2008), Chang & Chan (2009) use the vega–weighted net demand for volatility to determine whether volatility informed trading exists within the Taiwan options market. Their studies show that foreign institutional investors possess the strongest and most direct volatility information, which is realized by the delta–neutral options or futures trading. In addition, a few individual investors (less than 1% of individual trading) might be informed and use the strangle strategy.

Additionally, there are some empirical studies on the relation between the sentiment and realized volatility, such as Banerjee, Doran & Peterson (2007), Brown & Cliff (2004), Low (2004), Verma & Verma(2007), Wang, Keswani & Taylor (2006) support the significant incremental explanatory power of investor sentiment in the fitting and forecasting future volatility in multiple–factor model,

2.3 The Information Content of Options Volume and Put-Call Ratio

While less attention is given to the impact of options volume on the realized volatility or vice versa, the exact role of options volume is still a topic worth looking into. The existing literature also provides evidence on the information content of options trading volume for the future volatility. On the one hand, Kim & Kim (2004) use the daily volume and open interest as information variables to investigate the relationship between options trading and the volatility of the underlying asset. They argue that the unexpected volume increase is associated with the volatility increase while the unexpected open interest increase would lead to the volatility decrease. Ohk & Jang (2007) also examine the relation between the options volume and the volatility of KOSPI200 index. They classify investors into individual investors, institutional investors, bank and foreign investors. The result shows that the individual investors and the other investor group have the information about the future stock volatility. Comparing to the findings of Kim & Kim (2004), Blasco, Corredor & Santamaria (2010), Ohk & Jang (2007) show that options volume is hard to explain the volatility of underlying asset. However, they argue that the potential informed trading in the options market is channeled through out-of-money options rather than at-the-money options. On the other hand, some scholars argue that there is feedback relation between options volume and the future volatility. Such as Sarwar (2004), he uses the error components and dummy variable models to allow for the relations between volatility and volume to vary by the option's time-to-maturity and moneyness. The results suggest that previous call and put volumes have strong predictive ability with respect to the future price volatility. The results also indicate that the future price volatility has positive effect on the options volume, but that the rises and falls in volatility exert asymmetric influences on the option volume. Sarwar (2005) examines the dynamic relations between future price volatility of the S&P500 index and trading volume of S&P500 options to explore the informational role of options volume in predicting the price volatility. He finds that previous option volumes have strong predictive ability with respect to the future price volatility. Similarly, lagged changes in volatility have significant predictive power for options volume. Since there is no consensus among the empirical studies on this issue, which leaves us with some open theoretical and empirical issues. This paper revisits the issue on the informational role of options volumes for the volatility of index options because this research has access to a new dataset that promises new insights.

In addition, we use the put-call ratio as another information variable in this research to investigate the predictive power of options volume for the future volatility. In practice, the put-call ratio is frequently discussed in the financial press and is widely used by technical analysts as a short-term technical indicator of the investor sentiment concerning future equity price trends. Especially, many stock market experts cite the put-call ratio as an important indicator of investor sentiment, with a low (high) value indicating excessive optimism (pessimism). An increasing ratio is a clear indication that investors are starting to move toward instruments that gain when prices decline rather than when they rise.

There have been extensive studies published on the information content of put-call ratio. Simon & Wiggins III (2001) examine the predictive power of popular sentiment indicators, including the publicly observed put-call ratio, the volatility index, and the trading index for S&P500 futures returns. The empirical results indicate that these variables have statistically and economically significant forecasting power. Pan & Poteshman (2006) first define the non-publicly observable open-buy put-call ratio as the "information variable" and use it as a proxy for signed option volume to test the model of Easley, Hara & Srinivas(1998). They find that, in line with the informational and directional hypotheses of EOS model, equity option volume contains information about future stock price movements, and equity put-call ratio is a momentum signal. However, Chang, Hsieh & Lai (2009) do not find that options volume, as a whole, carries information on spot index returns using a dataset of Taiwan index options transaction records. While the open-buy put-call ratio on middle-horizon index options from foreign institutional investors has greater predictive power on the next-day index returns and is a momentum signal. These findings imply that the different directional impact of put-call ratio on spot index changes can result from differences in sophistication among investor types. Lin (2011) investigates the predictability of popular market-based sentiment indicator, the put-call ratio, for future stock price movements using the non-publicly unique and publicly observed stock index option volume obtained from the emerging Taiwan Futures Exchange. They find that the non-public put-call ratio contains information content about future stock index movements while the predictability of publicly observed put-call ratio is statistically insignificant. Additionally, their results show that the short-dated put-call ratio dominated by individual investors is a contrary spot market indicator while the long–dated put-call ratio dominated by foreign institutional investors is a momentum spot market indicator. Consequently, the findings provide additional evidence that the different directional impact of short- and long–dated put-call ratio can result from differences in sophistication among investor types. Unlike the previous works on the information content of put-call ratio for underlying asset return, this research is interested in the predictability of the put-call ratio for the future volatility of underlying asset.

2.4 The Informational Role of Various Investors

In this study, this study also investigates the informational role of various investor classifications. To acquire useful insight, previous researches regarding who would be informed traders are reviewed. Grinblatt & Keloharju (2000) and Kamesaka et al. (2003) report that foreign investors outperform domestic investors significantly in some stock markets such as in Finland and Japan. Their results imply that foreign investors are typically better informed traders than domestic investors in such markets. In addition, Dvorak (2005) compares the "per market transaction profit" of domestic market with that of foreign investors to examine which group of investors was more informed. Consistent with preceding notions, Froot, O'Connell & Seasholes (2001), Griffin, Nardari & Stulz (2004) and Richards (2005) provide the most relevant examinations of the relationship between such foreign investors capital flows and returns. Froot, O'Connell, & Seasholes (2001) find that foreign investors actually possess more information on stocks than domestic investors. Moreover, Richards (2005) finds comprehensive evidence to show that foreign capital flows have a positive correlation with host-country stock returns. In the same vein, Lin (2011) finds that open trading by foreign institutional investors conveys more information regarding the underlying index, and open selling of individual investors is more likely to introduce noise signals to the spot market. However, the information role of trading by domestic institutions on spot index returns is ambiguous.

Several of the prior studies have found that abnormal positive returns in Korea are associated with foreign inflows. Ohk (2008) finds that the cumulative return on stock investment of foreign investors is far more than that of domestic investors. The result of study can be explained by the information asymmetry between foreign investors and domestic investors. Both Griffin, Nardari & Stulz (2004) and Richards (2005) find that the capital flows from foreign institutional investors do indeed have significant predictive power with regard to next-day Korea spot index return, whereas flows from other types of investors appear to have no significant predictive power. With regard to the performance of foreigners relative to domestic investors, this study aims to document new and robust evidence on this issue in the Korean options market, which has not been explored fully in the existing published literature.

2.5 The Information Content of Options Moneyness

The existing literature also provides evidence on the influence of different levels of liquidity and degrees of leverage on informed traders' choice. De & Donders (1998) suggest informed traders use in-the-money (ITM) options to increase their trading profits because ITM options are more sensitive to underlying equity price changes than other options. Kaul, Nimalendran & Zhang (2004) argue that at-the-money (ATM) options are more liquid and more sensitive to volatility, and have lower bid-ask spreads than other options. ATM potions, thus, are most useful in predicting equity price movement. On the other hand, Chakravarty, Gulen & Mayhew (2005) show that out-of-the-money (OTM) options play the most significant role in the price discovery process among all options, because OTM options provide the highest leverage for investors. Hence, if information content of options varies with options' moneyness, pooling all options together could result in mixed findings. Following the suggestion of Easley, O'Hare & Srinivas (1998), this research attempts to explore the informed trading hypothesis by considering particular options series. A directional informed investor may make more by trading in the options contracts with the highest leverage (OTM), while investors trading on volatility will tend to concentrate on ATM options.

2.6 The Response of Options Volume to News Announcements

There is a common belief among academics and practitioners that economic conditions play a key role in asset pricing. Because macroeconomic news announcements can contain unexpected information about current economic conditions, they may result in changes in asset prices and market volatility. Further, because the value of index options is directly linked to market volatility, there may be movements in an options market when there is a macroeconomic news announcement. Moreover, if market participants anticipate the effect of news announcements, there may also be preceding changes in the options volume.

Before examining the impact of macroeconomic news announcements on options trading volume, it is worthwhile to take a look at the theoretical models related to scheduled news announcements. As discussed by Nofsinger & Prucyk (2003), various theoretical models make different assumptions and therefore they predict somewhat different reactions. One category of these models is information-based models, like that of Kim & Verrecchia (1991a), assuming that traders collect private information and trade according to their opinions before news announcement. After the announcement, increased volume and price changes are caused proportionally by the unexpected part of the news. In another model of Kim & Verrecchia (1991b) assume that the traders collect private information and that the information on the news is highly anticipated. They find that the variance declines as the quality of the announcement increases. One similar type of model has been proposed by Ederington & Lee (1996), who assume investors to gather private information, but that there still is some uncertainty before the announcement. Consequently, their result shows that volatility increases before and decreases after the announcement as the uncertainty is resolved by the market participants.

However, as the above models imply, no distinction is made between good and bad news. Barberis, Shleifer & Vishny (1998) create a behavioral model, in which it is assumed that good news is expected to be followed by good news and vice versa. This indicates that high (low) volatility will follow after bad (good) news. McQueen & Roley (1993) argue that unexpected positive news may not be good for the stock market because market participants consider not only the current positive situation but also the possibility of future downturns. Further, some behavioral models, like those of Shefrin & Statman (1985) and Hong & Stein (1999), suggest that investors trade and react differently after good vs. bad news announcements. These two models suggest that investors may trade after good news, but not after bad news and that the reaction is slower in the case of a bad news announcement. Nofsinger & Prucyk (2003) shows that most of high volume and high volatility after announcement come from the announcement that is considered bad news, while good news elicits lower volume and is not associated with high volatility. In summary, the theories provide a rich background for the empirical examination, suggesting an asymmetric effect between good and bad news.

A number of previous studies define the unexpected part of news as the difference between the anticipation and realization of the news. In the same vein, Äijö (2008) investigates the effect of scheduled US and UK macroeconomic news announcements on the return distribution implied by FTSE-100 option prices. The results provide new evidence for the whole implied return distribution being systematically affected by certain macroeconomic news announcements. After controlling the unexpected content of the news announcement for quality (good vs. bad news), it is found that good (bad) news causes implied volatility to decrease (increase), option-implied return distribution becomes less (more) left-skewed and kurtosis increases (decreases).

Although so many studies focus on the influence of news announcement on the volatility of underlying asset, there is little research on the influence of news announcement on options volume. This study tends to fill this void. This research attempts to link the options volume with the volatility to investigate whether the predictive power of options volume for the future volatility attributes to the informed trading rather than other purpose. Although the methodology of Äijö (2008) is used to examine the effects of news announcements, this study extends the methodology to investigate the effects more closely. Whereas Äijö (2008) uses daily data, the present study uses intraday data to examine shorter-term effects of news announcements. Many studies demonstrate that the effects of news announcements are incorporated by and disappear from markets very quickly. Therefore, intraday data should be used to obtain a more accurate timeline and measure the exact magnificence of the effects. Therefore, applied the methodology of Äijö (2008) to this research, a positive (negative) stock market return is regard as a sign of good (bad) news. Because the present study investigates the KOSPI200 index options market, it takes the daily log return for the KOSPI200 index as the stock market return. In addition, this study conducts the regression separately for good news and bad news to investigate whether the information content of options trading volume can be systematically explained by certain macroeconomic news announcement.

3 Hypothesis and Methodology

Much research has been devoted to modeling and forecasting the volatility of returns. Some of previous studies have approved that a negative shock to financial time series is likely to cause more volatility to rise than a positive shock of the same magnitude. Based on the existence of asymmetric response to the bad or good news, EGARCH (1,1) model is adopted to estimate the volatility of KOSPI200 index in this study.

3.1 The Relation Between Options Volume and the Volatility of KOSPI200 Index

The exponential GARCH model was proposed by Nelson (1991). There are various ways to express the conditional variance equation. One of these specifications is seen as below:

$$R_t = c + \sum_{i=1}^{10} R_{t-i} + \rho D_1 + \delta D_2 + \mu_t \qquad \mu_t = \sqrt{h_t}\,\varepsilon_t \tag{3-1}$$

$$ln\ (h_t) = \omega + \beta \ln(h_{t-1}) + \gamma \frac{\mu_{t-1}}{\sqrt{h_{t-1}}} + \alpha\left[\frac{|\mu_{t-1}|}{\sqrt{h_{t-1}}} - \sqrt{\frac{2}{\pi}}\right]) \tag{3-2}$$

Where R_t stands for the return of KOSPI200 index. To mitigate the impact of non-synchronous trading effects①, the dummy variable D_1 is used in this research. The dummy variable is 1 if the transaction occurs during the non-synchronous period, vice versa. Due to the occurrence of the subprime mortgage crisis② during the sample period, the dummy variable is also used in this research. The dummy variable is 1 during the subprime mortgage crisis period, vice versa.

The model has several advantages over the pure GARCH specification. First, Nelson & Cao (1992) argue that the nonnegativity constraints in the linear GARCH model are too restrictive. The GARCH model imposes the nonnegative constraints on the parameters, while there are no restrictions on these parameters in the EGARCH model. In the EGARCH model, since the ln (h_t) is modeled, then even if the parameters are negative, h_t will be positive. There is thus no need to artificially impose non-negativity constraints on the model parameters. Second, asymmetries are allowed for under the EGARCH formulation. The γ parameter measures the asymmetry or the leverage effect. If $\gamma = 0$, then the model is symmetric. When $\gamma < 0$, then positive shocks (good

---

① The Korea Exchange (KRX) opens at 09:00 KST and closes at 15:00 KST, but the options market opens at 09:00 KST and closes at 15:15 KST. It means there is competitive transaction time period in the Korean security markets, which brings the non-synchronous trading effects.

② According to the research of Choi (2011), June 1, 2008 is used as the dividing standard time of the subprime mortgage crisis in this research.

news) generate less volatility than negative shocks (bad news)①. When $\gamma > 0$, implies that positive innovations are more destabilizing than negative innovations.

To analyze the existence of informed trading in the Korean options market, firstly, the lead-lag relationship between options volumes and index volatility during the full sample period is examined. Vector Auto-regression (VAR) model is used to test whether the options volume (the volatility of KOSPI200 index) conveys information that is useful in predicting the volatility of KOSPI200 index (options volume). The VAR model is written as below:

$$VR_t = \alpha_0 + \sum_{i=1}^{10} \gamma_i VR_{t-i} + \sum_{i=1}^{10} \delta_i X_{t-i} + \omega_t \tag{3-3}$$

$$X_t = \alpha_0 + \sum_{i=1}^{10} \alpha_i X_{t-i} + \sum_{i=1}^{10} \beta_i VR_{t-i} + \pi_t \tag{3-4}$$

Where VR_t represents the volatility of KOSPI200 index returns, and X_t is the information variables which include options volume and put-call ratio respectively. This study adopts the information variable of Pan & Poteshman (2006), by assuming that the put-call ratio parsimoniously combines the information of the put and call volumes; it is therefore defined as:

$$PC_t = \frac{P_t}{P_t + C_t} \tag{3-5}$$

Where P_t and C_t are the volume of put and call options for KOSPI200 index. This variable has already been widely used in the literature as a proxy

---

① Ohk (1997) and Ku (2000) find the movement of stock in the bullish market is totally different from the movement in the bearish market, suggesting that there exists asymmetry in Korean security market.

of different investors has different impacts on the future movement of the underlying asset. The information based model constructed by Easley, O'Hara & Srinivas (1998), is capable of investigating the linkage between options volume and stock prices. However, they use aggregated options trading ignoring difference between various types of investors. Instead, to acquire useful insight regarding hypothesis on the informational role of various investor classification, Eq.(3-6) and(3-7) are respectively applied to domestic institutional investor, individual investors, foreign institutional investors. Based on the findings of the previous researches, the options volume of foreign investors is expected to have greatest influence on the future volatility of KOSPI200 index in Korean security markets.

$$\mathrm{VR}_t = \alpha_0 + \sum_{i=1}^{10} \gamma_i \mathrm{VR}_{t-i} + \sum_{i=1}^{10} \delta_i X_{t-i}^{IC} + \omega_t \tag{3-6}$$

$$X_t^{IC} = \alpha_0 + \sum_{i=1}^{10} \alpha_i X_{t-i}^{IC} + \sum_{i=1}^{10} \beta_i \mathrm{VR}_{t-i} + \pi_t \tag{3-7}$$

Where VR_{t-i}^{IC} represents the volatility of KOSPI200 index, and X_{t-i}^{IC} denotes the information variables for different investors.

H3: The null hypothesis is that regardless of investor classifications, the information variable X_{t-i}^{IC} has no influence on the volatility of KOSPI200 index.

H4: The null hypothesis is that the volatility of KOSPI200 index has no influence on the options volume, regardless of investor classifications.

3.3 The Information Content of Options Moneyness

The previous studies also show options with different degrees of

either for private information or investors' heterogeneous beliefs. Be following the methodology of Bessembinder & Seguin (1992), the volume and put-call ratio are divided into expected and unex components according to the ARIMA (10, 0, 10) method. The ex component of the options volume reflects forecastable part based historical data. The unexpected component of the options volume difference of the real options volume and expected component, interpre shock to market change.

Eq. (3 - 3) tests whether lagged information variables x_{t-i} le volatility of KOSPI200 index (VR_t). Eq. (3-4) examines whether VR_{t-i} convey information regarding the behavior of options market cont for lagged information variable. The optimal number of lags in Eq.(3- (3-4) is determined by the Akaike Information Criterion(AIC)①.

H1: The null hypothesis is that the spot and options markets ar separating equilibrium. Namely, the information variable x_{t-i} has no inf on the future volatility of KOSPI200 index.

H2: The null hypothesis is that the volatility of KOSPI200 index influence on the options volume.

3.2 The Informational Role of Various Investo

This empirical investigations focus on whether the options trading

---

① Lag 10 is determined as the optimal lag according to the Akaike information c moneyness have various influence on informed investors when making the choice. For instance, although out-of-the-money (OTM) options provide investors with more leverage, they also tend to involve higher delta-to-premium ratios, due to higher bid-ask spread and commissions. On the other hand, ATM options expose informed investors to higher volatility risk (vega) and bid-ask spread of at-the-money options tends to be lower, so investors trading on volatility tend to concentrate their trading in ATM options. In the light of this literature, it appears reasonable to suspect that trading volume in all positions can mask different intentions among investors trading in options with different degrees of moneyness. This study also attempts to explore the information content of options volume by considering particular options series. Directional-informed investors are expected to prefer the options contracts with the highest leverage (OTM), while volatility-informed trader will tend to concentrate on ATM options.

$$VR_t = \alpha_0 + \sum_{i=1}^{10} \gamma_i VR_{t-i} + \sum_{i=1}^{10} \delta_i X_{t-i}^M + \omega_t \quad (3-8)$$

$$X_t^M = \alpha_0 + \sum_{i=1}^{10} \alpha_i X_{t-i}^M + \sum_{i=1}^{10} \beta_i VR_{t-i} + \pi_t \quad (3-9)$$

Where VR_{t-i} represents the volatility of KOSPI200 index, X_{t-i}^M denotes the information variables for different options moneyness.

H5: The null hypothesis is that no matter options' moneyness, the information variable X_{t-i}^M has no influence on the future volatility of KOSPI200 index.

H6: The null hypothesis is that the volatility of KOSPI200 index has no influence on options volume of the different options' moneyness.

3.4 The Response of Options Volume to News Announcements

It should be stressed that the results obtained in the previous section are not only related with the fact that options trading volume may reflect an information effect, but also with the fact that it may be due to transactions made for liquidity or hedging purposes. To investigate this issue, a direct test of the influence of news released as direct measures of information on unexpected trading volume is performed.

$$UX_t^* = \theta_0 + \sum_{i=-12}^{-1} \theta_{t+i} \times \mathrm{GN}_{t+i} + \sum_{i=0}^{12} \tau_{t+i} \times \mathrm{GN}_{t+i} + \rho_1 R_t + \varepsilon_t \quad (3\text{-}10)$$

$$UX_t^* = \theta_0 + \sum_{i=-12}^{-1} \theta_{t+i} \times \mathrm{BN}_{t+i} + \sum_{i=0}^{12} \tau_{t+i} \times \mathrm{BN}_{t+i} + \rho_2 R_t + \varepsilon_t \quad (3\text{-}11)$$

$$UX_t^* = VX_t^* - E(\frac{VX_t^*}{\phi_{t-1}}), \quad E\left(\frac{VX_t^*}{\phi_{t-1}}\right) = ARIMA(10,0,10) \quad (3\text{-}12)$$

Where $UX_t{}^*$ stands for the unexpected volume of options; VX_t^* denotes the real options volume. Expected volume is estimated by means of ARIMA (10,0,10) to find the best fit for the data. GN_t and BN_t represent the good and bad news respectively.

Many previous researches attest to the importance of macroeconomic news announcements as informational events in the equity and options market. This analysis adds to this body of literature by addressing time variation in the level of informational asymmetry surrounding these announcements. In particular, this study provides empirical evidence to link time variation in informational asymmetry directly to time variation in options trading volume. To determine whether the predictive power of options volume for the future volatility comes from informational asymmetry, this study takes advantage of the fact that the non-informational trading is insensitive to the level of informational asymmetry, while the information - based trading depends on the level of informational asymmetry in a crucial way.

In order to investigate directly for the presence or absence of informed trading in the options market, it seems more correct to relate, not trading volume, but unexpected volume to news. Surprise in variable, namely an error term, is used to test for the existence of informed trading in options market. The variable denotes total options volume and put-call ratio. Event time $t=0$ stands for the time that the news announcement occurs. Event time $t= \pm i$ is the 5-mintues interval i periods before or after announcement. GN_t represents the dummy variable for good news and BN_t represents the dummy variable for bad news. Following the methodology of Nofsinger (2003), macroeconomic news announcements are classified as good news and bad news according to the KOSPI200 index return on the actual time of the announcement.

In order to investigate whether the predictive power of options volume for the future volatility of index is attributed for the informed trading, six important macroeconomic news announcements each for South Korea and U.S. are selected as exogenous information events. They include gross domestic product (GDP), employment report (EMP), consumer price index (CPI), producer price index (PPI), industrial production index (IPI) and trade balance (TB). In order to avoid misleading conclusions if option investors simply respond to movements in the underlying market in a "trend-following" way, it is necessary to include the underlying asset return along the trading session as an additional explanatory variable.

H7: The null hypothesis is that there is no reaction of unexpected options volume to scheduled macroeconomic news before the news is announced.

However, if informed trading exists in the index options market, the options volume should yield significant reactions before the news announcements。Hypotheses in this research are summarized as follows:

Table 3-1 Research Hypotheses

	Null Hypothesis
Relation between options volume and the volatility of KOSPI200 index	H1: The null hypothesis is that the information variable x_{t-i} has no influence on the future volatility of spot index
	H2: The null hypothesis is that the volatility of KOSPI200 index has no influence on the options volume
Informational role of various investors	H3: The null hypothesis is that the information variable X_{t-i}^{IC} has no influence on the volatility of spot index regardless of investor classifications
	H4: The null hypothesis is that the volatility of spot index has no influence on the options volume of various investors regardless of investor classifications
Information content of options moneyness	H5: The null hypothesis is that no matter options' moneyness, the information variable X_{t-i}^{M} has no influence on the future volatility of spot index
	H6: The null hypothesis is that no matter options' moneyness, the volatility of spot index has no influence on options volume of the different options' moneyness
The response of unexpected options volume to news announcement	H7: The null hypothesis is that there is no reaction of unexpected options volume to scheduled macroeconomic news before the news is announced

4 Dataset

4.1 KOSPI200 Index Options

The options dataset used in this study was obtained from the Korea Exchange (KRX) database. Despite its relatively short history, KOSPI200 index options market has become one of the largest options markets in the world. Table 4-1 shows that the KOSPI200 index options is the most actively traded index options in the world. The KOSPI200 index is a capitalization-weighted index of 200 blue-chip stocks representing the Korean stock market and industry groups. European-style options on the KOSPI200 index have been traded on the KRX since 1997. KOSPI200 index options have a contract size of KRW 100,000 per index point① and a minimum price movement of 0.05 (when the premium is greater than 3 index points) or 0.01 (when the

① After March 9, 2012, KOSPI200 index options have a contract size of KRW 500,000 per index point. But in the sample period of this research, KOSPI200 index options still have a contract size of KRW 100,000 per index.

premium is 3 index points or less) index point. Maturity dates and last trading days are the second Thursday of three consecutive near-term delivery months and one additional month from the quarterly cycle (March, June, September and December).

The sample period spans from January 2, 2007 to December 31, 2008. Unique dataset of this study consists of all KOSPI200 options transaction records, the identification of investors, investors classes, type of options (call or put), option characteristics (strike price and time to expiration), trading directions (buy or sell), transaction prices and volume during the sample period. Instead of the daily options data used in the previous studies on the informational content of the options volume for the future volatility, 5-min intraday data are utilized in this research. The data used in the empirical tests is filtered according to the following criteria:

a. To avoid the systematic bias arising from the lack of liquidity, options with more than 60 days to expiration are removed.

b. Five-minute data were sorted from the minute-by-minute data of options prices. As it was necessary to use actual traded options data, only those data are adopted where an actual transaction occurred. These options volume are not equal to that occurring five minutes previously.

Table 4-1 The World's Top 5 Derivative Contracts

Rank	Contract	2007	2008	2009	2010
1	KOSPI200 Options, KRX	2 709	2 766	1 375	1 671
2	E-mini S&P500 Futures, CME	415	633	299	308
3	DJ Euro Stoxx 50 Futures, EUREX	327	432	178	205

Table 4-1 (continued)

Rank	Contract	2007	2008	2009	2010
4	DJ Euro Stoxx 50 Options, EUREX	251	400	158	152
5	SPDR S&P500 ETF Options	141	321	181	219

Notes: This table shows the ten most active derivative contracts, measured in millions of contracts from 2007 to 2010; the rank is based on the trading volume for 2007.

Source: Futures Industry Association (www.futuresindustry.org).

One of the unique features of dataset in this study is that each transaction record can be identified for different investor classes, which enables us to classify the associated transaction volume into three main investor classifications: domestic institutional investors, foreign institutional investors, individual investors.

Options volume and put-call ratio are used as information variables in this study. Following Pan & Poteshman (2006), Put-Call ratio is the key variable in the examination of the information content of options trading volume, which is defined as $P_t/(P_t + C_t)$. P_t and C_t are the volume of put and call options for KOSPI200 index respectively. This variable has already been widely used in the literature as a proxy either for private information or investors' heterogeneous beliefs.

In addition, 2% and 6% differences between strike and underlying prices are used as cut-off points of the categories of moneyness. The moneyness of options is classified by the S/K values (where S is the underlying asset price and K is the strike price). ATM options refer to S/K values in the range of 0.98~1.02. Call options with S/K values in the range of 0.94~0.98 or put options with S/K values in the range of 1.02 ~ 1.06 are classified as OTM options. Call options with S/K values below 0.94 or put options with S/K values above 1.06 are classified as deep OTM options. Call options with S/K values in the range of 1.02 ~ 1.06 or put options with S/K values in the range of 0.94 ~ 0.98 are classified as ITM. Finally, put options with S/K values below 0.94 or call options above 1.06 are classified as deep ITM.

Table 4 - 2 summaries the statistics for KOSPI200 index options. As shown in the table 4-2, the trading volume of put options by individuals far exceeds the levels of trading by domestic securities firms or by foreign investors. Individuals are often regarded as unsophisticated investors who trade mostly for reasons unrelated to information. For example, Barber, Lee, Liu & Odean (2007), Barber & Odean (2000), and Grinblatt & Keloharju (2000) find that individual investors are uninformed, liquidity traders. With the abundance of uninformed individual traders in the market, sophisticated investors would find it easier to capitalize on their superior information-processing skills and/or their superior trading skills. It is believable that ample liquidity and the dominant participation by individual investors in the KOSPI200 options market provide an ideal setting to test for the presence of information-motivated trading. In addition, table 4 - 2 shows that domestic individual investors and institutional investors prefer call options to put options, by contrast, foreign investors are more interested in put options. Moreover, regardless of call options and put options, the trading volumes of out-of-the-money options are far more than the other options. The trading volumes of deep out-of-the-money rank only second to out-of-the-money, which accounts for the low premium and high leverage of these options.

Table 4-2 Descriptive Statistics for KOSPI200 Index Options Market

		Mean	Max.	Min.	Std.	Skew.	Kurt.
Call options	Deep ITM options	396. 143 5	8 958 343	0	49 889. 440 0	175. 094 1	31 359. 130 0
	ITM options	578. 829 5	345 091	0	2 732. 975 0	64. 222 04	7 174. 249 0
	ATM options	13 630. 740 0	986 303	0	30 228. 180 0	6. 495 4	102. 041 5
	OTM options	59 033. 660 0	1. 26E+09	0	6 573 970	192. 296	36 980. 170 0
	Deep OTM options	306 827. 400 0	2. 64E+09	0	22 738 120	88. 355 7	8 353. 003 0
Put options	Deep ITM options	219. 317 8	1 577 483	0	12 159. 080 0	107. 438 5	12 257. 250 0
	ITM options	1 516. 264 0	41 169 166	0	214 075. 100 0	192. 292 1	36 979. 170 0
	ATM options	17 102. 830 0	540 195	0	36 432. 090 0	4. 196 6	26. 521 7
	OTM options	31 802. 250 0	575 774	3	36 627. 980 0	2. 522 1	13. 469 1
	Deep OTM options	110 382. 600 0	1. 42E+09	0	9 414 009	131. 339 1	18 031. 250 0
Call options	Institutional investors	66 550. 610 0	1 009 700	203	61 879. 020 0	2. 403 7	13. 506 2
	Foreign investors	34 639. 320 0	273 385	139	25 773. 710 0	1. 716 3	7. 679 9
	Individual investors	59 430. 070 0	606 118	1 825	47 601. 310 0	2. 238 9	10. 669 5
Put options	Institutional investors	45 623. 710 0	734 621	12	47 199. 610 0	3. 083 5	19. 359 5
	Foreign investors	36 125. 410 0	307 664	108	24 698. 570 0	1. 578 7	7. 048 8
	Individual investors	48 181. 560 0	511 488	714	39 617. 750 0	2. 425 0	12. 353 7

4. 2 Macroeconomic Variables

In order to investigate whether the unexpected trading volume are related to the the news announcement from Korea and U. S., six macroeconomic variables from Korea and U. S respectively are selected, based on earlier literature. These major economic indicators are included as follows: Producer Price Index (PPI), gross domestic product (GDP), employment report

(EMP), consumer price index (CPI), industrial production index (IDP) and trade balance (TB).

Table 4-3 List of Macroeconomic News Announcements

Announcement	Abbreviation	Time	Number of Good News	Number of Bad News	Number of All News
Korea					
Gross domestic product	KGDP	08:00	7	1	8
Employment report	KEMP	13:30	10	14	24
Consumer price index	KCPI	13:30	11	13	24
Producer price index	KPPI	12:00	12	12	24
Industrial production index	KIP	13:30	13	11	24
Trade balance	KTB	08:00	12	10	22
U.S.					
Gross domestic product	USGDP	22:30	15	9	24
Employment report	USEMP	22:30	13	11	24
Consumer price index	USCPI	22:30	16	8	24
Producer price index	USPPI	22:30	14	10	24
Industrial production index	USIPI	23:15	15	9	24
Trade balance	USTB	22:30	14	10	24

All Korean news announcements are obtained from Statistic Korea. The US news announcements are collected from the Economic Calendar on Yahoo's pages①. The Korea Exchange (KRX) opens at 09:00 KST and closes at

① Http://www.biz.yahoo.com/calendar/.

15:00 KST. Because U.S. news is announced after the KRX is closed, this study assumes the announcement time of U.S. news to be 09:00 KST the next day. Korean news is announced at different times because of the different time schedules of the authorities. In the cases of EMP, CPI and IND in South Korea, the official announcement time are 13:30 KST. In addition, the official announcement times of GDP and TB in South Korea are 08:00 KST. The announced time of PPI is 12:00. To make inference from how option markets response to the macroeconomic news announcement, this paper follows Nofsinger & Prucyk (2003) and regard positive (negative) KOSPI200 stock market return as good(bad) news.

5 Empirical Analysis

As shown in Table 5 - 1, the null hypothesis of normal distribution for KOSPI200 index return can be rejected according to the p-value. Not withstanding, the value of skewness is negative, which means that the distribution of KOSPI200 index return is a long fat tail distribution. Based on these descriptive statistics, it is reasonable that EGARCH model is the optimal approach to estimate the volatility of KOSPI200 index return.

Table 5-1 Descriptive Statistics of KOSPI200 Index Return

Mean	Median	Max.	Min.	Std.	Skew.	Kurt.	Jarque-bera	p-value
-6. 29e-06	0. 000 0	0. 071 3	-0. 066 4	0. 002 5	-1. 205 2	111. 502 2	18 151 232	0. 000 0

Because VAR model requires that all variables should be stationary, it is necessary to test whether all variables in this research are stationary by unit root test. Augmented Dickey-Fuller test is used in this study. As shown in Table 5 - 2, the test statistics of all variables are significant, so the null hypothesis of a unit root can be rejected.

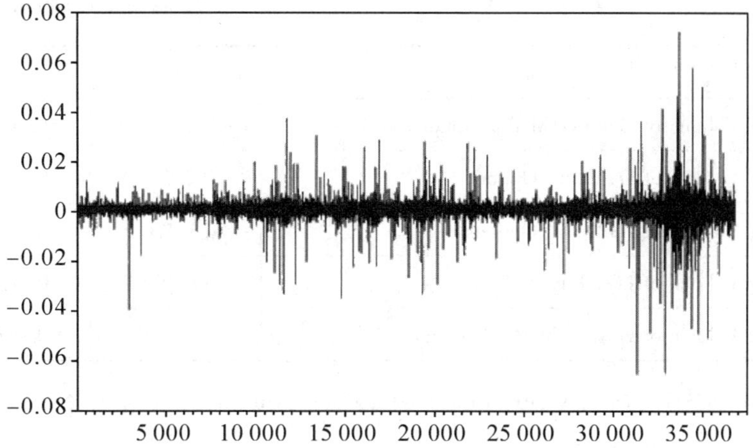

Figure 5−1 The Return of KOSPI200 Index

Table 5−2 Results for Unit Root Test of Variables in VAR Model

Variable	t−statistics	p−value
Volatility Estimated from EGARCH(1,1)	−14.245 5	0.000 0
Trading Volume of Call Options	−12.914 5	0.000 0
Trading Volume of Put Options	−12.765 7	0.000 0
Trading Volume of Call Options for Individual Investors	−12.769 3	0.000 0
Trading Volume of Call Options for Institutional Investors	−12.743 0	0.000 0
Trading Volume of Call Options for Foreign Investors	−12.476 6	0.000 0
Trading Volume of Put Options for Individual Investors	−12.624 3	0.000 0
Trading Volume of Put Options for Institutional Investors	−12.233 7	0.000 0
Trading Volume of Put Options for Foreign Investors	−14.381 3	0.000 0
Trading Volume of Deep OTM Call Options	−192.325 6	0.000 1
Trading Volume of OTM Call Options	−11.142 1	0.000 0
Trading Volume of ATM Call Options	−12.873 8	0.000 0
Trading Volume of ITM Call Options	−192.305 9	0.000 1
Trading Volume of Deep ITM Call Options	−182.096 4	0.000 1

Table 5-2 (continued)

Variable	t-statistics	p-value
Trading Volume of Deep OTM Put Options	-192. 340 1	0. 000 1
Trading Volume of OTM Put Options	-192. 316 8	0. 000 1
Trading Volume of ATM Put Options	-13. 520 5	0. 000 0
Trading Volume of ITM Put Options	-17. 160 7	0. 000 0
Trading Volume of Deep ITM Put Options	-181. 959 5	0. 000 1

The critical values of 1%,5%,10% for unit root test are-3. 430 357,-2. 861 427,-2. 566 750.

Before investigating the relation between options volumes and the volatility of KOSPI200 index, it is necessary to estimate the volatility of the KOSPI200 index using EGARCH (1, 1) model. 10 is determined as the optimal lag length according to Akaike's information criterion. As reported in panel A of Table 5-3, the coefficient of mean equation is significant at 5% level until lag 5. The coefficients of dummy variable D_1 and D_2 are significant at 5% level, suggesting it is necessary to control the influence of non-synchronous effect and subprime mortgage crisis. Coefficient estimates for the variance equation are given in the panel B. The asymmetry term in EGARCH (1, 1) is statistically significant and the coefficient estimate is negative, suggesting that negative return shock will imply a higher next period conditional variance than positive return shock of the same magnitude. The other coefficient estimates in the panel B are also significant. Figure 5-2 shows the conditional variance estimated from EGARCH (1,1).

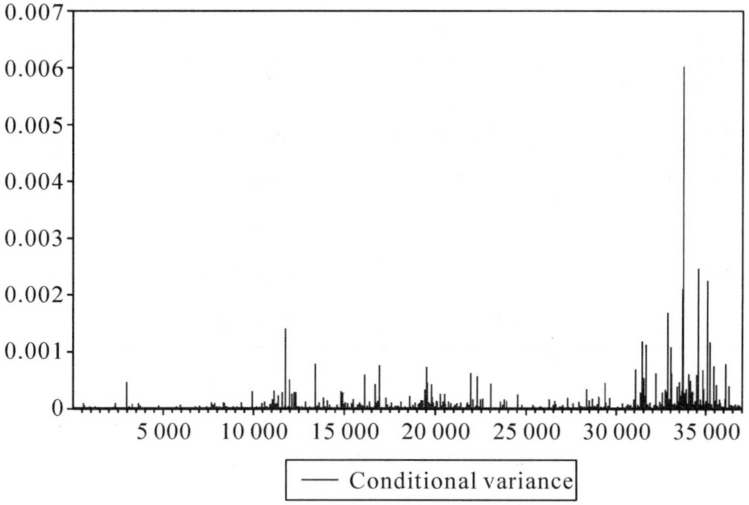

Figure 5-2 Conditional Variance Estimated from EGARCH (1,1)

Table 5-3 Results for Mean Equation and Variance Equation in EGARCH (1,1)

Panel A: Mean Equation			
Variable	Coefficient	Std. Error	Prob.
C	0. 000 1	0. 000 0	0. 000 0
R_{t-1}	0. 282 4	0. 001 8	0. 000 0
R_{t-2}	-0. 198 6	0. 001 6	0. 000 0
R_{t-3}	0. 032 3	0. 001 4	0. 000 0
R_{t-4}	-0. 008 4	0. 001 8	0. 000 0
R_{t-5}	-0. 001 9	0. 002 2	0. 391 6
R_{t-6}	0. 012 9	0. 002 0	0. 000 0
R_{t-7}	0. 009 2	0. 002 3	0. 000 0
R_{t-8}	0. 002 7	0. 002 4	0. 253 0
R_{t-9}	-0. 001 1	0. 002 4	0. 635 1
R_{t-10}	0. 003 1	0. 002 3	0. 181 5
ρ	0. 000 0	0. 000 0	0. 002 9
δ	-0. 001 1	0. 000 0	0. 000 0

Table 5-3 (continued)

Panel B: Variance Equation			
Variable	Coefficient	Std. Error	Prob.
ω	-1.353 9	0.020 1	0.000 0
β	0.645 9	0.005 3	0.000 0
γ	-0.109 3	0.004 0	0.000 0
α	0.930 7	0.001 4	0.000 0

5.1 The Relation Between Options Volumes and the Volatility of KOSPI200 Index

Table 5-4 reports the results of the relation between the overall options volume and the future volatility of KOSPI200 index. As reported in the table, the results of call options are broadly in agreement with the results of put options in terms of the direction of the effects of lagged volatilities (volumes) on volume (volatility) under the Vector Autoregressive method. The results show the effect of call and put options volume on the volatility is significant from lag 5 to lag 10. Compared to the result of put options, the call volumes have a relatively stronger predictive power for the future price volatility. On the other hand, for either calloption or put option, this study finds that the volatility of KOSPI200 has significant predictive ability with respect to the options volume only at lag 1. This finding confirms that there is contemporary feed-back relation between the volatility and options volume, although the relation is not strong as expected. The result of put-call ratio is different from the result of put and call options. The coefficient of put-call ratio is only significant at lag 9 and lag 10. However, there is no significant effect of the volatility on the put-call ratio. Because of unexpected options volume as the surprise in volume, it is beneficial to capture the activity of informed trader with private information. It is necessary to further investigate the relation between the options volume and the future volatility using the unexpected options volume as dependent variable instead of options volume in VAR analysis. Based on the method of ARIMA (10,0,10), the options volume is divided into expected volume and unexpected volume. Expected volumes stand for the activity of investors with the public information based on the historical data. Unexpected volumes represent the activity of informed trader with private information.

Table 5-5 shows the relation between the unexpected options volumes and the volatility of KOSPI200 index. As reported in the table, all the coefficients for the influence of the volatility on the unexpected options volume are insignificant, where we can see that the future volatility of underlying asset does not lead the unexpected options volumes. However, the influence of the unexpected options volume on the volatility is totally different. Comparing to the result of Table 5-4, it is obviously that most of the coefficients for the influence of the unexpected call and put options volume on the volatility are greater and more significant. This result shows that the unexpected options volume have stronger and more significant predictive power for the volatility. This finding provides distinct evidence on the existence of informed

Table 5-4 Results for the Relation between the Options Volumes and the Volatility of the KOSPI200 Index

Dependent Variable: VR_t				Dependent Variable: VOL_t			
	Call	Put	Put-Call Ratio		Call	Put	Put-Call Ratio
Vol_{t-1}	-4. 43E-10***	-5. 44E-10***	-0. 000 1	VR_{t-1}	-807 516. 800***	-548 457. 900 0***	-0. 224 773
Vol_{t-2}	-3. 21E-10**	0. 000 0	0. 000 1	VR_{t-2}	163 557. 200 0	-25 164. 640 0	-0. 406 8
Vol_{t-3}	0. 000 0	0. 000 0	-0. 000 1	VR_{t-3}	-123 560. 900 0	-77 117. 380 0	0. 153 7
Vol_{t-4}	0. 000 0	0. 000 0	-0. 000 1	VR_{t-4}	60 958. 300 0	103 638. 700 0	-0. 403 5
Vol_{t-5}	0. 000 0	0. 000 0	0. 000 1	VR_{t-5}	-253 113. 000 0	-92 464. 560 0	0. 325 1
Vol_{t-6}	6. 16E-10***	5. 76E-10***	-0. 000 1	VR_{t-6}	112 844. 700 0	-62 645. 190 0	-0. 058 6
Vol_{t-7}	4. 39E-10***	4. 72E-10***	0. 000 0	VR_{t-7}	-85 108. 870 0	-183 595. 000 0	-0. 231 0
Vol_{t-8}	5. 90E-10***	6. 86E-10***	0. 000 0	VR_{t-8}	211 237. 000 0	49 271. 370 0	-0. 486 2
Vol_{t-9}	2. 10E-09***	2. 22E-09***	-0. 000 2***	VR_{t-9}	261 827. 700 0	314 504. 800 0	-0. 345 9
Vol_{t-10}	-8. 34E-10***	-1. 53E-09***	-0. 000 6***	VR_{t-10}	-600 285. 600 0	-563 671. 900 0	-0. 127 9

Table 5-4 (continued)

Dependent Variable: VR_t				Dependent Variable: VOL_t			
	Call	Put	Put-Call Ratio		Call	Put	Put-Call Ratio
VR_{t-1}	0. 773 6***	0. 780 1***	0. 780 1***	Vol_{t-1}	0. 467 5***	0. 477 0***	0. 398 1***
VR_{t-2}	0. 040 06***	0. 041 0***	0. 041 1***	Vol_{t-2}	0. 065 6***	0. 071 8***	0. 110 6***
VR_{t-3}	-0. 050 3***	-0. 049 6***	-0. 049 8***	Vol_{t-3}	0. 075 0***	0. 077 7***	0. 070 7***
VR_{t-4}	0. 008 7	0. 008 8	0. 007 4***	Vol_{t-4}	0. 060 6***	0. 066 8***	0. 048 6***
VR_{t-5}	0. 002 8	0. 004 0	0. 003 1	Vol_{t-5}	0. 035 3***	0. 033 5***	0. 058 1***
VR_{t-6}	0. 014 7***	0. 015 2**	0. 014 6**	Vol_{t-6}	0. 046 8***	0. 038 4***	0. 033 8***
VR_{t-7}	0. 016 1***	0. 016 2***	0. 015 1**	Vol_{t-7}	0. 028 8***	0. 025 2***	0. 031 7***
VR_{t-8}	-0. 000 6	0. 000 0	-0. 000 3	Vol_{t-8}	0. 023 7***	0. 020 9***	0. 026 2***
VR_{t-9}	-0. 001 4	-0. 000 9	-0. 001 5	Vol_{t-9}	0. 030 0***	0. 032 2***	0. 030 0***
VR_{t-10}	0. 051 2	0. 051 5	0. 046 9	Vol_{t-10}	0. 056 7***	0. 056 7***	0. 037 7***

***, ** and * denote the significant level of 1%, 5%, and 10% respectively.

Table 5-5　Results for VAR Analysis of Unexpected Information Variables for Put and Call Options

Dependent Variable: VR_t				Dependent Variable: VOL_t			
	Call	Put	Put-Call Ratio		Call	Put	Put-Call Ratio
Vol_{t-1}	0. 000 0	-3. 46E-10**	0. 000 0	VR_{t-1}	-420 586. 700 0	-313 820. 800 0	0. 071 6
Vol_{t-2}	-3. 00E-10**	-4. 35E-10***	0. 000 1	VR_{t-2}	75 534. 640 0	-118 085. 900 0	-0. 277 2
Vol_{t-3}	0. 000 0	0. 000 0	0. 000 0	VR_{t-3}	-111 427. 900 0	-67 965. 680 0	0. 261 7
Vol_{t-4}	2. 76E-10**	0. 000 0	-0. 000 1	VR_{t-4}	-205 138. 900 0	103 626. 200 0	-0. 253 6
Vol_{t-5}	3. 23E-10***	0. 000 0	0. 000 1	VR_{t-5}	-302 981. 400 0	-106 879. 700 0	0. 444 8
Vol_{t-6}	1. 00E-09***	8. 20E-10***	0. 000 0	VR_{t-6}	418 795. 800 0	63 815. 410 0	0. 029 9
Vol_{t-7}	1. 32E-09***	1. 18E-09***	0. 000 0	VR_{t-7}	-178 185. 200 0	-95 839. 900 0	-0. 125 6
Vol_{t-8}	1. 68E-09***	1. 63E-09***	0. 000 0	VR_{t-8}	-7 357. 919 0	-108 690. 900 0	-0. 360 7
Vol_{t-9}	3. 33E-09***	3. 47E-09***	-0. 000 2***	VR_{t-9}	282 307. 200 0	227 053. 900 0	-0. 238 4
Vol_{t-10}	3. 02E-09***	2. 71E-09***	-0. 000 2***	VR_{t-10}	-828 336. 900 0	-247 372. 300 0	0. 276 8

Table 5-5 (continued)

Dependent Variable: VR_t				Dependent Variable: VOL_t			
	Call	Put	Put-Call Ratio		Call	Put	Put-Call Ratio
VR_{t-1}	0.757 5***	0.769 4***	0.784 7***	Vol_{t-1}	-0.001 9	-0.001 0	0.000 0
VR_{t-2}	0.047 0***	0.045 2***	0.041 9***	Vol_{t-2}	-0.001 7	-0.000 5	0.000 8
VR_{t-3}	-0.046 5***	-0.047 3***	-0.049 2***	Vol_{t-3}	-0.000 8	-0.002 0	-0.001 5
VR_{t-4}	0.011 0	0.010 0	0.008 3	Vol_{t-4}	0.002 0	0.002 4	-0.002 5
VR_{t-5}	0.007 2	0.006 1	0.004 1	Vol_{t-5}	-0.007 3	-0.000 3	0.004 0
VR_{t-6}	0.017 1***	0.017 0***	0.015 3**	Vol_{t-6}	-0.003 3	-0.005 0	0.001 1
VR_{t-7}	0.018 9***	0.017 4***	0.016 0***	Vol_{t-7}	-0.008 2	-0.006 3	0.004 2
VR_{t-8}	0.001 9	0.001 1	0.000 3	Vol_{t-8}	-0.007 0	-0.004 9	-0.003 9
VR_{t-9}	-0.000 7	-0.000 7	-0.000 9	Vol_{t-9}	0.005 7	0.012 8	0.000 3
VR_{t-10}	0.057 1	0.053 3***	0.049 8	Vol_{t-10}	0.014 6	0.016 3	0.000 7

***, ** and * denote the significant level of 1%, 5%, and 10% respectively.

trading. In addition, the result for the put-call ratio further confirms that the options volume leads the volatility. In summary, the results of Table 5-4 and Table 5-5 indicate that the predictive power of unexpected options volume for the future volatility is much stronger than the options volume, consistent with prediction of this research. Thus, the unexpected volume of put and call appears to provide advance signals to investors about the forthcoming short-run movements in the expected future volatility of the KOSPI200 index.

5.2 The Informational Role of Various Investors

Reviewing the previous studies, it is commonly believed that different investors have diverse information on the future movement of the spot index. Thus the influence of various investors on the future volatility of the spot index is greatly different. So it is necessary to investigate the information role of various investors in Korean security markets. In this research, the investors are divided into three classifications: foreign investors, individual investors and institutional investors. Table 5-6 indicates the results for VAR analysis of call options of various investors. As shown in the Table 5-6, foreign investors have strongest predictive power on the future volatility of KOSPI200 index among various investors, less strong but appreciable for institutional investors, and weaker but still significant for individual investors. On the contrary, using the options volume as dependent variable, the coefficient estimates for the volatility on the options volume for various investors are insignificant except at lag1. It is obviously that the influence of the volatility on the options volume is not strong as the impact of the options volume on the volatility. In order to unearth who may be informed traders, it is necessary to investigate the influence of the unexpected call options volume on the volatility of the spot index.

Table 5-7 shows the results for VAR analysis of unexpected volume of call options of various investors. Compared with the findings of the Table 5-6, the parameter and statistic significance in Table 5-7 is much higher than the same statistic in Table 5 - 6, suggesting that the predictive power of unexpected call options volume is stronger than that of call options volume. When the volatility of the spot index is used as dependent variable, there is no doubt that the foreign investors have strongest and more significant predictive ability with respect to the future price volatility by comparing the coefficients of statistics. Not withstanding, the unexpected call options volumes of institutional investors and individual investors have significant predictive power on the volatility of KOSPI200 index. Oppositely, when the unexpected call options volumes is used as the dependent variable, there is no significant reaction of the unexpected call options volume to the lag volatility except for institutional investor at lag1, suggesting that the volatility of the spot index have no predictive power on the unexpected call options volume for various investor.

Table 5-6　Results for VAR Analysis of Call Options Volume of Various Investors

Dependent Variable: VR_t				Dependent Variable: VOL_t			
	Individual investor	Foreign investor	Institutional investor		Individual investor	Foreign investor	Institutional investor
Vol_{t-1}	−8. 78E−10***	0. 000 0	−2. 82E−10**	VR_{t-1}	−538 735. 500 0***	−306 067. 900 0***	−712 327. 900 0***
Vol_{t-2}	−5. 50E−10***	0. 000 0	−3. 02E−10**	VR_{t-2}	−29 836. 720 0	247 649. 3***	149 443. 100 0
Vol_{t-3}	0. 000 0	0. 000 0	0. 000 0	VR_{t-3}	71 745. 220 0	−115 351. 100 0	−207 899. 000 0
Vol_{t-4}	0. 000 0	7. 90E−10***	0. 000 0	VR_{t-4}	16 283. 170 0	120 159. 600 0	−37 825. 570 0
Vol_{t-5}	−3. 97E−10*	3. 54E−09***	0. 000 0	VR_{t-5}	−234 633. 200 0	−134 446. 300 0	−130 980. 800 0
Vol_{t-6}	5. 25E−10***	3. 10E−09***	4. 59E−10***	VR_{t-6}	154 914. 800 0	137 290. 000 0	−36 095. 840 0
Vol_{t-7}	0. 000 0	2. 37E−09***	3. 65E−10***	VR_{t-7}	−180 953. 000 0	−57 559. 650 0	12 630. 650 0
Vol_{t-8}	6. 14E−10***	2. 34E−09***	4. 74E−10***	VR_{t-8}	223 383. 400 0	168 667. 200 0	70 399. 050 0
Vol_{t-9}	3. 47E−09***	8. 20E−09***	1. 05E−09***	VR_{t-9}	162 686. 300 0	91 991. 850 0	279 469. 900 0
Vol_{t-10}	0. 000 0	−5. 76E−09***	−6. 85E−10***	VR_{t-10}	−393 611. 600 0	−213 246. 600 0	−606 033. 800 0

Table 5-6 (continued)

Dependent Variable: VR_t				Dependent Variable: VOL_t			
	Individual investor	Foreign investor	Institutional investor		Individual investor	Foreign investor	Institutional investor
VR_{t-1}	0.770 4***	0.748 9***	0.781 4***	Vol_{t-1}	0.465 2***	0.531 2***	0.421 6***
VR_{t-2}	0.041 1***	0.035 8***	0.041 1***	Vol_{t-2}	0.082 5***	0.020 4***	0.077 9***
VR_{t-3}	-0.050 1***	-0.053 2***	-0.049 5***	Vol_{t-3}	0.078 7***	0.085 1***	0.066 4***
VR_{t-4}	0.008 8	0.007 1	0.008 7	Vol_{t-4}	0.058 7***	0.045 1***	0.073 3***
VR_{t-5}	0.003 5	-0.001 9	0.003 5	Vol_{t-5}	0.034 2***	0.042 3***	0.035 8***
VR_{t-6}	0.014 6**	0.011 1*	0.015 6***	Vol_{t-6}	0.050 9***	0.037 0***	0.047 1***
VR_{t-7}	0.016 2***	0.013 1*	0.016 3***	Vol_{t-7}	0.029 8***	0.029 5***	0.030 2***
VR_{t-8}	2.41E-05	-0.003 0	-0.000 3	Vol_{t-8}	0.014 9***	0.017 8***	0.037 1***
VR_{t-9}	-0.001 8	-0.005 3	-0.000 4	Vol_{t-9}	0.030 0***	0.030 0***	0.028 1***
VR_{t-10}	0.051 6	0.042 6	0.051 4**	Vol_{t-10}	0.053 7***	0.044 6***	0.058 9***

***, ** and * denote the significant level of 1%, 5%, and 10% respectively.

Table 5-7 Results for VAR Analysis of Unexpected Call Options Volume of Various Investors

Dependent Variable: VR_t				Dependent Variable: VOL_t			
	Individual investor	Foreign investor	Institutional investor		Individual investor	Foreign investor	Institutional investor
Vol_{t-1}	-3.86E-10**	0.000 0	0.000 0	VR_{t-1}	-193 611.300 0	-63 392.950 0	-451 917.6**
Vol_{t-2}	-4.81E-10***	0.000 0	0.000 0	VR_{t-2}	-189 267.700 0	189 524.100 0	221 433.300 0
Vol_{t-3}	-3.95E-10**	8.03E-10**	2.40E-10*	VR_{t-3}	-88 956.620 0	-245 233.600 0	-129 045.800 0
Vol_{t-4}	0.000 0	1.17E-09***	3.84E-10***	VR_{t-4}	102 387.300 0	82 191.050 0	-170 648.300 0
Vol_{t-5}	0.000 0	1.33E-09***	3.28E-10***	VR_{t-5}	-267 967.000 0	-156 801.700 0	-239 240.400 0
Vol_{t-6}	7.79E-10***	3.91E-09***	8.13E-10***	VR_{t-6}	85 485.420 0	153 950.900 0	52 627.690 0
Vol_{t-7}	1.07E-09***	4.36E-09***	1.13E-09***	VR_{t-7}	-90 059.210 0	10 566.120 0	-63 427.450 0
Vol_{t-8}	1.68E-09***	5.10E-09***	1.38E-09***	VR_{t-8}	136 138.600 0	130 098.100 0	-48 830.690 0
Vol_{t-9}	4.87E-09***	1.10E-08***	2.14E-09***	VR_{t-9}	23 624.970 0	-17 147.790 0	360 102.800 0
Vol_{t-10}	5.15E-09***	6.02E-09***	1.90E-09***	VR_{t-10}	-435 169.800 0	-225 758.200 0	-761 538.500 0

Table 5-7 (continued)

Dependent Variable: VR_t				Dependent Variable: VOL_t			
	Individual investor	Foreign investor	Institutional investor		Individual investor	Foreign investor	Institutional investor
VR_{t-1}	0.758 0***	0.748 2***	0.770 6***	Vol_{t-1}	-0.001 9	-0.000 7	-0.001 7
VR_{t-2}	0.051 7***	0.046 6***	0.043 1***	Vol_{t-2}	-0.002 6	-0.015 8***	-0.001 5
VR_{t-3}	-0.046 0***	-0.047 8***	-0.047 8***	Vol_{t-3}	0.003 9	0.008 3	-0.001 4
VR_{t-4}	0.010 8	0.010 9	0.009 8	Vol_{t-4}	0.000 3	0.025 2***	0.000 7
VR_{t-5}	0.008 0	0.006 6	0.005 3	Vol_{t-5}	-0.013 4	0.022 4**	0.001 3**
VR_{t-6}	0.017 2***	0.017 1	0.016 3***	Vol_{t-6}	-0.002 3	0.006 9	-0.004 3***
VR_{t-7}	0.017 9***	0.018 7***	0.017 7***	Vol_{t-7}	0.001 0	0.000 6	-0.007 7
VR_{t-8}	0.001 4	0.001 1	0.001 5	Vol_{t-8}	-0.013 7	0.001 1	-0.006 5
VR_{t-9}	-0.000 8	-0.000 7	0.000 0	Vol_{t-9}	-0.004 4	0.007 2	-0.004 4
VR_{t-10}	0.055 0	0.056 3	0.055 0	Vol_{t-10}	0.008 9	0.001 3	0.005 8

***, ** and * stand for the significant level of 1%, 5%, and 10% respectively.

Next, the lead-lag relation between the put options volumes of various investors and the volatility of spot index is examined respectively. Table 5-8 shows the results for VAR analysis of put options volume of various investors. Firstly, incontrast to the Table 5-6, the predictive power of the put options volume for volatility is not stronger than that of the call options volume. Secondly, when the volatility of the spot index is used as dependent variable, it is obviously that the influence of put options volume of foreign investor on the volatility is much stronger than that of institutional and individual investors. In addition, the put options volumes of institutional investors have significant effect on the volatility of KOSPI200 index. The put options volumes of individual investors have predictive power on the volatility of KOSPI200 index at lag 1, lag 2, lag 4, lag 8, lag 9 and lag 10. Conversely, when the put options volumes are used as the dependent variable, the volatility only at lag 1 has a significant effect on the put options volumes of various investors. This finding shows that there is a contemporary feed-back relation between put options volume for various investors and the volatility of KOSPI200 index respectively.

Table 5-9 shows the linkage between unexpected put options volumes for various investors and the volatility of KOSPI200 index. The parameters and statistic significance of Table 5-9 are much higher than the same statistic in Table 5-8, confirming that the predictive power of unexpected put options volume is stronger than that of overall options volume. When the volatility of the spot index are used as dependent variable, coefficients for the influence of unexpected put options volume of foreign investor on the volatility are significant from the forth to the tenth time interval, which indicate that the unexpected put options volumes of foreign investors continuously lead the volatility of the spot index by 35 minutes (7 * 5min). In addition, the unexpected put options volumes of institutional investors and individual investors lead the volatility of the spot index by 30 minutes (6 * 5min) and 25 minutes respectively. It is obviously that the influence of unexpected put options volume of foreign investors on the volatility is much stronger than that of institutional and individual investors in terms of the value of coefficients and statistic significance. Conversely, when the unexpected put options volumes is used as the dependent variable, all the coefficient estimates are insignificant except individual investors at lag 1, suggesting that the volatility of the spot index has no impact on the unexpected put options volume for institutional and foreign investors. In summary, by the examination of the information content of unexpected put options volume for various investors, this study finds foreign investors indeed have stronger predicted power on the future volatility of spot index than institutional investors and individual investors. Moreover, regardless of foreign investors, individual investors and institutional investors, the unexpected put volumes contain the information about the forthcoming short-run movements in the expected future volatility of the KOSPI200 index.

Table 5-8 Results for VAR Analysis of Put Options Volume of Various Investors

Dependent Variable: VR_t				Dependent Variable: VOL_t			
	Individual investor	Foreign investor	Institutional investor		Individual investor	Foreign investor	Institutional investor
Vol_{t-1}	-8. 36E-10***	0. 000 0	-6. 13E-10***	VR_{t-1}	-455 980. 000 0***	-248 665. 400 0***	-331 937. 200 0***
Vol_{t-2}	-6. 52E-10***	0. 000 0	0. 000 0	VR_{t-2}	-13 812. 760 0	118 855. 900 0	-109 337. 400 0
Vol_{t-3}	0. 000 0	0. 000 0	0. 000 0	VR_{t-3}	-19 465. 940 0	-54 025. 230 0	-79 807. 830 0
Vol_{t-4}	-4. 96E-10*	0. 000 0	0. 000 0	VR_{t-4}	100 908. 300 0	87 052. 160 0	24 811. 600 0
Vol_{t-5}	0. 000 0	7. 48E-10**	0. 000 0	VR_{t-5}	-108 935. 200 0	-117 444. 000 0	14 352. 760 0
Vol_{t-6}	0. 000 0	2. 49E-09***	0. 000 0	VR_{t-6}	-78 607. 940 0	87 519. 640 0	-114 388. 900 0
Vol_{t-7}	0. 000 0	1. 74E-09***	0. 000 0	VR_{t-7}	-111 340. 100 0	-108 132. 700 0	-146 208. 700 0
Vol_{t-8}	6. 11E-10***	2. 29E-09***	5. 19E-10***	VR_{t-8}	9 404. 862 0	108 682. 600 0	24 704. 490 0
Vol_{t-9}	3. 95E-09***	5. 75E-09***	9. 20E-10***	VR_{t-9}	269 506. 200 0	26 421. 230 0	290 741. 500 0
Vol_{t-10}	-1. 13E-09***	-6. 80E-09***	-7. 27E-10***	VR_{t-10}	-356 071. 800 0	-275 531. 000 0	-447 658. 300 0

Table 5-8 (continued)

Dependent Variable: VR_t				Dependent Variable: VOL_t			
	Individual investor	Foreign investor	Institutional investor		Individual investor	Foreign investor	Institutional investor
VR_{t-1}	0.778 4***	0.769 5***	0.783 9***	Vol_{t-1}	0.469 0***	0.541 7***	0.420 3***
VR_{t-2}	0.040 9***	0.041 4***	0.041 4***	Vol_{t-2}	0.087 6***	0.022 1***	0.095 1***
VR_{t-3}	-0.049 6**	-0.050 0***	-0.049 4***	Vol_{t-3}	0.077 2***	0.070 1***	0.083 2***
VR_{t-4}	0.008 7	0.009 3	0.008 4	Vol_{t-4}	0.068 9***	0.058 7***	0.072 0***
VR_{t-5}	0.004 2	0.002 5	0.004 1	Vol_{t-5}	0.038 7***	0.023 9***	0.038 5***
VR_{t-6}	0.015 2***	0.013 8**	0.015 7***	Vol_{t-6}	0.038 5***	0.040 6***	0.039 7***
VR_{t-7}	0.016 4***	0.015 5**	0.016 0***	Vol_{t-7}	0.014 9***	0.019 6***	0.040 5***
VR_{t-8}	-0.000 3	-0.001 0	0.000 1	Vol_{t-8}	0.029 7***	0.020 0***	0.017 3***
VR_{t-9}	-0.000 8	-0.002 2	-0.000 6	Vol_{t-9}	0.034 1***	0.037 9***	0.025 9***
VR_{t-10}	0.051 7	0.050 6	0.050 7	Vol_{t-10}	0.047 3	0.040 6***	0.067 9***

***, ** and * stand for the significant level of 1%, 5%, and 10% respectively.

Table 5-9 Results for VAR Analysis of Unexpected Put Options Volume of Various Investors

Dependent Variable: VR_t				Dependent Variable: VOL_t			
	Individual investor	Foreign investor	Institutional investor		Individual investor	Foreign investor	Institutional investor
Vol_{t-1}	-4.48E-10*	0.000 0	0.000 0	VR_{t-1}	-270 147.4**	-85 055.410 0	-123 029.300 0
Vol_{t-2}	-5.24E-10**	0.000 0	0.000 0	VR_{t-2}	-23 391.650 0	160 398.700 0	-148 685.300 0
Vol_{t-3}	0.000 0	0.000 0	0.000 0	VR_{t-3}	-68 575.340 0	-67 185.580 0	-86 802.430 0
Vol_{t-4}	0.000 0	1.12E-09***	0.000 0	VR_{t-4}	87 225.500 0	13 383.940 0	-1 715.819 0
Vol_{t-5}	0.000 0	1.84E-09***	5.42E-10***	VR_{t-5}	-109 112.200 0	-57 418.880 0	10 833.110 0
Vol_{t-6}	7.25E-10***	3.68E-09***	8.65E-10***	VR_{t-6}	-123 455.500 0	199 771.8**	-41 041.380 0
Vol_{t-7}	1.19E-09***	4.50E-09***	1.09E-09***	VR_{t-7}	-144 924.200 0	-175 151.2*	-133 360.000 0
Vol_{t-8}	1.84E-09***	5.75E-09***	1.50E-09***	VR_{t-8}	21 763.230 0	-50 355.260 0	-97 334.380 0
Vol_{t-9}	5.77E-09***	9.66E-09***	2.25E-09***	VR_{t-9}	291 034.2**	-10 399.930 0	220 382.100 0
Vol_{t-10}	4.85E-09***	5.52E-09***	2.36E-09***	VR_{t-10}	-458 774.200 0	-366 600.600 0	-406 529.300 0

Table 5-9 (continued)

Dependent Variable: VR_t				Dependent Variable: VOL_t			
	Individual investor	Foreign investor	Institutional investor		Individual investor	Foreign investor	Institutional investor
VR_{t-1}	0.764 8***	0.751 1***	0.776 5***	Vol_{t-1}	-0.002 0	-0.002 6	-0.001 7
VR_{t-2}	0.049 3***	0.045 6***	0.042 5***	Vol_{t-2}	-0.001 9	-0.001 3	-0.002 5
VR_{t-3}	-0.046 6***	-0.045 8***	-0.048 3***	Vol_{t-3}	-0.002 5	-0.000 8	0.002 4
VR_{t-4}	0.010 4	0.011 343*	0.008 9	Vol_{t-4}	0.003 7	0.002 6	0.008 3
VR_{t-5}	0.006 8	0.007 2	0.005 0	Vol_{t-5}	-0.006 6	-0.009 5*	-0.007 3
VR_{t-6}	0.016 8***	0.017 8***	0.016 8***	Vol_{t-6}	-0.005 0	-0.011 7**	-0.010 3**
VR_{t-7}	0.017 1***	0.017 8***	0.016 9***	Vol_{t-7}	-0.006 7	-0.012 1***	-0.004 7
VR_{t-8}	0.001 6	0.000 2	0.000 8	Vol_{t-8}	-0.005 3	0.006 1	-0.011 2**
VR_{t-9}	0.000 0	-0.001 3	0.000 1	Vol_{t-9}	-0.002 6	0.024 0	-0.003 3
VR_{t-10}	0.054 1	0.057 8	0.052 9	Vol_{t-10}	0.007 3	0.011 7	0.013 6

*** , ** and * stand for the significant level of 1% , 5%, and 10% respectively.

In the following section, the put-call ratio is used as the information variable to examine the lead-lag relation between the options volumes for various investors and the volatility of KOSPI200 index. Pan & Poteshman (2006) argue that put-call ratio as the useful indicator of the information trading in the options market, contains the information about the future direction of the underlying asset. Therefore, it is reasonable to infer that the put-call ratio is beneficial to investigate the information content of the options volume of various investors for the volatility of KOSPI200 index. Table 5-10 shows the relation between put-call ratio for various investors and the volatility of KOSPI200 index. Firstly, this study finds that the predictive power of put-call ratio of foreign investors and institutional investors on the volatility are significant at lag 9 and lag 10 respectively. In contrast to foreign investors, the put-call ratios of individual investors have shorter but significant effect on the volatility of KOSPI200 index; while this study finds that there is no significant effects of the volatility on the put-call ratios of all investors.

Table 5-11 shows the results for VAR analysis of unexpected put-call ratio of various investors. The findings are similar to the results of Table 5-10, while the parameters and statistic significance are slightly higher, suggesting that the predictive power of unexpected put-call ratio is stronger than that of overall put-call ratio. When the volatility of KOSPI200 index is used as dependent variable, this study finds that the predictive power of the unexpected put-call ratio for the volatility of spot index is strongest for foreign investors, less strong but appreciable for institutional investors. On the contrary, when the unexpected put-call ratio is used as the dependent

Table 5–10 Results for VAR Analysis of Put-Call Ratio of Various Investors

Dependent Variable: VR_t				Dependent Variable: PC_t			
	Individual investor	Foreign investor	Institutional investor		Individual investor	Foreign investor	Institutional investor
PC_{t-1}	0. 000 0	0. 000 0	−0. 000 1	VR_{t-1}	−0. 469 7	−0. 241 0	−0. 011 9
PC_{t-2}	0. 000 1	0. 000 0	0. 000 1	VR_{t-2}	0. 056 9	−0. 650 0	−0. 752 2
PC_{t-3}	0. 000 0	0. 000 0	−0. 000 1	VR_{t-3}	−0. 128 5	0. 209 7	0. 205 7
PC_{t-4}	−0. 000 1	−0. 000 1	0. 000 0	VR_{t-4}	−0. 129 5	−0. 615 0	−0. 215 6
PC_{t-5}	0. 000 1	0. 000 1	0. 000 1	VR_{t-5}	0. 105 7	0. 178 0	0. 632 1
PC_{t-6}	−0. 000 1	−0. 000 1	0. 000 0	VR_{t-6}	−0. 477 7	0. 109 0	−0. 241 5
PC_{t-7}	0. 000 0	0. 000 0	0. 000 0	VR_{t-7}	0. 025 4	−0. 586 1	0. 297 2
PC_{t-8}	−0. 000 1	−0. 000 1	0. 000 0	VR_{t-8}	−0. 624 9	−0. 023 7	−0. 726 4
PC_{t-9}	−0. 000 1	−0. 000 2***	−0. 000 1**	VR_{t-9}	−0. 040 6	−0. 699 3	−0. 741 4
PC_{t-10}	−0. 000 7***	−0. 000 8***	−0. 000 2***	VR_{t-10}	−0. 014 4	−0. 626 3	0. 630 6

Table 5-10（continued）

Dependent Variable: VR_t				Dependent Variable: PC_t			
	Individual investor	Foreign investor	Institutional investor		Individual investor	Foreign investor	Institutional investor
VR_{t-1}	0.780 5***	0.776 4***	0.783 8***	PC_{t-1}	0.392 0***	0.344 8***	0.389 8***
VR_{t-2}	0.040 8***	0.040 3***	0.041 3***	PC_{t-2}	0.122 9***	0.118 6***	0.104 5***
VR_{t-3}	-0.049 7***	-0.050 2***	-0.049 5***	PC_{t-3}	0.079 3***	0.082 1***	0.066 6***
VR_{t-4}	0.007 2	0.006 6	0.008 2	PC_{t-4}	0.058 6***	0.056 2***	0.046 1***
VR_{t-5}	0.003 3	0.002 6	0.003 6	PC_{t-5}	0.052 7***	0.057 6***	0.059 1***
VR_{t-6}	0.014 6**	0.013 5**	0.015 4**	PC_{t-6}	0.032 1***	0.047 1***	0.035 2***
VR_{t-7}	0.015 1**	0.014 3**	0.015 6***	PC_{t-7}	0.032 4***	0.035 7***	0.025 3***
VR_{t-8}	-0.000 4	-0.001 0	0.000 0	PC_{t-8}	0.029 5***	0.030 4***	0.027 1***
VR_{t-9}	-0.001 4	-0.001 9	-0.000 9	PC_{t-9}	0.024 8***	0.039 2***	0.025 8***
VR_{t-10}	0.046 6	0.043 9	0.049 3	PC_{t-10}	0.042 2***	0.042 8***	0.036 2***

***, ** and * stand for the significant level of 1%, 5%, and 10% respectively.

Table 5-11 Results for VAR Analysis of Unexpected Put-Call Ratio of Various Investors

Dependent Variable: VR_t				Dependent Variable: PC_t			
	Individual investor	Foreign investor	Institutional investor		Individual investor	Foreign investor	Institutional investor
PC_{t-1}	0. 000 0	0. 000 0	-0. 000 1	VR_{t-1}	-0. 182 2	0. 245 5	0. 108 6
PC_{t-2}	0. 000 1	0. 000 1	0. 000 1	VR_{t-2}	0. 182 0	-0. 424 4	-0. 668 1
PC_{t-3}	0. 000 0	0. 000 0	-0. 000 1	VR_{t-3}	-0. 027 5	0. 360 9	0. 297 0
PC_{t-4}	-0. 000 1	0. 000 0	-0. 000 1	VR_{t-4}	-0. 024 7	-0. 438 6	-0. 153 2
PC_{t-5}	0. 000 1	0. 000 1	0. 000 0	VR_{t-5}	0. 229 1	0. 392 5	0. 692 2
PC_{t-6}	0. 000 0	0. 000 0	0. 000 0	VR_{t-6}	-0. 377 5	0. 260 6	-0. 170 4
PC_{t-7}	0. 000 0	0. 000 0	0. 000 0	VR_{t-7}	0. 148 0	-0. 387 2	0. 342 8
PC_{t-8}	0. 000 0	-7. 51E-05**	0. 000 0	VR_{t-8}	-0. 538 2	0. 124 1	-0. 617 4
PC_{t-9}	-0. 000 1	-0. 000 2***	-0. 000 1***	VR_{t-9}	0. 045 3	-0. 553 2	-0. 685 5
PC_{t-10}	-0. 000 7	-0. 001 0***	-0. 000 2***	VR_{t-10}	0. 374 6	-0. 002 2	0. 891 8

Table 5-11 (continued)

Dependent Variable: VR_t				Dependent Variable: PC_t			
	Individual investor	Foreign investor	Institutional investor		Individual investor	Foreign investor	Institutional investor
VR_{t-1}	0. 784 2***	0. 785 0***	0. 785 1***	PC_{t-1}	0. 000 3	−0. 000 1	0. 000 1
VR_{t-2}	0. 041 9***	0. 041 6***	0. 041 6***	PC_{t-2}	−0. 001 3	0. 000 1	0. 000 7
VR_{t-3}	−0. 048 8***	−0. 049 1***	−0. 049 4***	PC_{t-3}	0. 001 2	0. 000 2	−0. 001 9
VR_{t-4}	0. 008 2	0. 008 1	0. 008 5	PC_{t-4}	0. 001 1	0. 000 2	−0. 000 7
VR_{t-5}	0. 004 5	0. 004 3	0. 003 8	PC_{t-5}	0. 003 3	0. 000 2	0. 006 5
VR_{t-6}	0. 015 1**	0. 015 4**	0. 015 6***	PC_{t-6}	−0. 001 3	−0. 000 7	0. 002 4
VR_{t-7}	0. 016 1***	0. 016 0***	0. 015 9***	PC_{t-7}	−0. 002 4	−0. 000 6	−0. 000 1
VR_{t-8}	0. 000 3	0. 000 2	0. 000 2	PC_{t-8}	−0. 002 8	0. 000 2	−0. 006 9
VR_{t-9}	−0. 000 6	−0. 000 7	−0. 000 7	PC_{t-9}	−0. 001 3	−0. 000 1	−0. 003 7
VR_{t-10}	0. 049 6***	0. 049 6***	0. 049 9***	PC_{t-10}	−0. 003 6	0. 003 3	0. 001 3

***, ** and * stand for the significant level of 1%, 5%, and 10% respectively.

variable, all the coefficient estimators are insignificant, suggesting that the volatility of KOSPI200 index has no impact on the unexpected put-call for various investors. These findings are similar as the result of unexpected call and put options volumes. In summary, by the examination of the information content of unexpected put-call ratio of various investors, this research not only finds that foreign investors indeed have strongest predicted power on the future volatility of KOSPI200 index, but also confirms the existence of the information asymmetry .

5. 3 The Information Content of Options Moneyness

Since options delta, vega, and leverage could determine the informed traders' choice, it is probable that the relations between option volume and volatility may vary with the option's moneyness. Table 5-12 shows the results for VAR analysis of call options of different moneyness. As indicated in the table 5-12, when the volatility of KOSPI200 index is used as the dependent variable in VAR analysis, the coefficients of call ATM options at lag 9 and lag 10 are statistically significant, coupled with the weaker but significant effect for OTM options. However, the estimators for deep OTM and ITM are significant only at lag 10. On the other hand, the volatility of ITM options, ATM options and OTM options only at lag 1 have significant and positive effect on the call volumes respectively. In order to further test the information content of options moneyness, it is necessary to test the relation between unexpected call options volume of different options moneyness and the volatility of KOSPI200 index.

Table 5-13 shows the results for VAR analysis of unexpected call options volume of different moneyness. In contrast to the Table 5-12, the parameters and statistic significance of Table 5-13 are much higher, suggesting that the predictive power of unexpected call options volume is stronger than that of call options volume. When the volatility of the spot index is used as the dependent variable in VAR analysis, this research finds that the influence of unexpected options volume of OTM options to the volatility is strongest and most significant, coupled with the weaker but significant effect for ATM options. Given these results in Table 5-13, it is reasonable to conjecture that the information content of options moneyness is different. Specially, because of lower premiums and higher leverage of OTM options, informed traders are more favorable to execute their trading using OTM options rather than ATM and/or ITM options. This finding is the same as the results of Chakravarty et al. (2004), who argue that informed traders prefer OTM options to maximize their profit. On the other hand, using the unexpected call options volumes as the dependent variable in VAR analysis, the volatility of ITM options, ATM options and OTM options only at lag 1 have significant effect on the call volumes respectively.

Table 5-12 Results for VAR Analysis of Call Options of Different Moneynes

Dependent Variable: VR_t						Dependent Variable: VOL_t					
	Deep OTM	OTM	ATM	ITM	Deep ITM		Deep OTM	OTM	ATM	ITM	Deep ITM
Vol_{t-1}	0.000 0	-7.43E-10***	0.000 0	0.000 0	0.000 0	VR_{t-1}	-12 131 123.000 0	-329 216.100 0***	-180 824.200 0***	4 615 307.000 0***	-30 540.210 0
Vol_{t-2}	0.000 0	0.000 0	0.000 0	0.000 0	0.000 0	VR_{t-2}	41 421 440.000 0	-36 922.750 0	68 816.550 0	-2 782 504**	94 956.170 0
Vol_{t-3}	0.000 0	0.000 0	0.000 0	0.000 0	0.000 0	VR_{t-3}	-9 967 273.000 0	-79 524.050 0	-56 737.660 0	-1 077 155.000 0	-54 938.320 0
Vol_{t-4}	0.000 0	0.000 0	0.000 0	0.000 0	0.000 0	VR_{t-4}	-27 266 606.000 0	30 875.680 0	46 762.300 0	779 552.900 0	-97 998.360 0
Vol_{t-5}	0.000 0	0.000 0	0.000 0	0.000 0	0.000 0	VR_{t-5}	19 951 418.000 0	-97 128.100 0	-80 825.060 0	-76 012.030 0	52 460.410 0
Vol_{t-6}	0.000 0	0.000 0	0.000 0	0.000 0	0.000 0	VR_{t-6}	17 759 918.000 0	-71 525.190 0	-37 858.640 0	-561 397.000 0	-82 167.460 0
Vol_{t-7}	0.000 0	0.000 0	0.000 0	0.000 0	0.000 0	VR_{t-7}	-23 546 508.000 0	-40 581.980 0	46 152.620 0	-148 876.600 0	7 640.011 0
Vol_{t-8}	0.000 0	0.000 0	0.000 0	0.000 0	0.000 0	VR_{t-8}	-7 485 560.000 0	25 496.370 0	-880.440 5	-15 894.720 0	-110.803 1
Vol_{t-9}	0.000 0	1.96E-09***	2.24E-09***	0.000 0	0.000 0	VR_{t-9}	2 265 314.000 0	35 329.460 0	65 070.930 0	43 822.090 0	26 334.410 0
Vol_{t-10}	1.36E-12***	-1.11E-09***	-1.55E-09***	9.06E-11***	0.000 0	VR_{t-10}	-5 059 853.000 0	-255 283.7***	-161 168.000 0	60 544.930 0	-14 624.650 0

Table 5-12 (continued)

Dependent Variable: VR_t						Dependent Variable: VOL_t					
	Deep OTM	OTM	ATM	ITM	Deep ITM		Deep OTM	OTM	ATM	ITM	Deep ITM
VR_{t-1}	0.785 340***	0.784 5***	0.785 4***	0.785 4***	0.814 5***	Vol_{t-1}	-0.000 1	0.437 3***	0.563 3***	-0.000 4	-0.000 1
VR_{t-2}	0.041 397***	0.041 2***	0.041 2***	0.041 4	0.034 0***	Vol_{t-2}	-0.000 1	0.077 9***	0.071 9***	0.000 1	0.000 0
VR_{t-3}	-0.049 284***	-0.049 4***	-0.049 4***	-0.049 1***	-0.063 8***	Vol_{t-3}	-0.000 1	0.084 1***	0.087 7***	-0.000 1	0.000 0
VR_{t-4}	0.008 3	0.008 4	0.008 3	0.008 4	0.001 3	Vol_{t-4}	-0.000 1	0.076 5***	0.064 8***	0.000 0	0.000 0
VR_{t-5}	0.003 9	0.003 9	0.004 0	0.003 9	0.008 9	Vol_{t-5}	-0.000 1	0.049 8***	0.039 7***	0.000 0	0.000 0
VR_{t-6}	0.015 721***	0.015 5***	0.015 5***	0.015 7***	0.014 7**	Vol_{t-6}	-0.000 1	0.051 4***	0.034 4***	0.000 1	-0.000 1
VR_{t-7}	0.015 8***	0.015 9***	0.015 9***	0.015 9***	0.004 7	Vol_{t-7}	-0.000 1	0.027 9***	0.025 9***	0.000 1	0.000 0
VR_{t-8}	0.000 0	-0.000 1	0.000 0	-0.000 2	-0.001 8	Vol_{t-8}	-0.000 1	0.023 6***	-0.006 9	0.000 0	0.000 0
VR_{t-9}	-0.000 5	-0.000 7	-0.000 6	-0.000 5	0.012 8*	Vol_{t-9}	-0.000 1	0.022 6***	0.011 8***	0.000 0	0.000 0
VR_{t-10}	0.049 8***	0.050 3***	0.049 7***	0.049 6***	0.006 6	Vol_{t-10}	-0.000 1	0.062 2***	0.057 6	0.000 0	-0.000 1

***, ** and * stand for the significant level of 1%, 5%, and 10% respectively.

Table 5-13 Results for VAR Analysis of Unexpected Call Options of Different Moneyness

Dependent Variable: VR_t						Dependent Variable: VOL_t					
	Deep OTM	OTM	ATM	ITM	Deep ITM		Deep OTM	OTM	ATM	ITM	Deep ITM
Vol_{t-1}	0.000 0	0.000 0	0.000 0	0.000 0	0.000 0	VR_{t-1}	-12 276 539.000 0	-217 041.8**	-177 944.9**	4 431 942***	-47 523.550 0
Vol_{t-2}	0.000 0	0.000 0	0.000 0	0.000 0	0.000 0	VR_{t-2}	41 385 954.000 0	-2 053.167 0	63 387.010 0	-2 827 204***	91 470.760 0
Vol_{t-3}	0.000 0	0.000 0	0.000 0	0.000 0	0.000 0	VR_{t-3}	-9 993 180.000 0	-59 460.480 0	-26 207.330 0	-1 115 391.000 0	-57 850.300 0
Vol_{t-4}	0.000 0	0.000 0	0.000 0	0.000 0	0.000 0	VR_{t-4}	-27 303 488.000 0	-12 733.850 0	28 906.120 0	729 681.800 0	-102 052.700 0
Vol_{t-5}	0.000 0	0.000 0	0.000 0	0.000 0	0.000 0	VR_{t-5}	19 913 308.000 0	-110 181.000 0	-88 111.640 0	-126 953.800 0	48 187.500 0
Vol_{t-6}	0.000 0	8.01E-10***	0.000 0	0.000 0	0.000 0	VR_{t-6}	17 723 846.000 0	4 982.542 0	-10 573.420 0	-612 374.400 0	-86 441.570 0
Vol_{t-7}	0.000 0	1.39E-09***	0.000 0	0.000 0	0.000 0	VR_{t-7}	-23 583 552.000 0	-51 585.140 0	10 915.370 0	-198 855.600 0	3 564.739 0
Vol_{t-8}	0.000 0	1.74E-09***	0.000 0	0.000 0	2.50E-10***	VR_{t-8}	-7 512 778.000 0	-70 741.080 0	-18 360.760 0	-54 353.820 0	-3 000.111 0
Vol_{t-9}	0.000 0	3.47E-09***	2.78E-09***	0.000 0	0.000 0	VR_{t-9}	2 231 887.000 0	92 016.580 0	86 697.540 0	-2 201.441 0	22 828.970 0
Vol_{t-10}	1.36E-12***	3.29E-09***	2.26E-09***	8.59E-11***	0.000 0	VR_{t-10}	-5 177 850.000 0	-268 692.3***	-160 106.8**	-122 447.100 0	-31 825.790 0

Table 5-13 (continued)

Dependent Variable: VR_t						Dependent Variable: VOL_t					
	Deep OTM	OTM	ATM	ITM	Deep ITM		Deep OTM	OTM	ATM	ITM	Deep ITM
VR_{t-1}	0.785 3***	0.777 1***	0.783 5***	0.785 4***	0.814 5***	Vol_{t-1}	0.000 0	-0.002 1	-0.000 5	-0.000 5	-0.000 1
VR_{t-2}	0.041 4***	0.043 3***	0.042 3***	0.041 4***	0.034 0***	Vol_{t-2}	0.000 0	-0.001 7	-0.000 7	-0.000 1	-0.000 1
VR_{t-3}	-0.049 3***	-0.048 2***	-0.049 0***	-0.049 3***	-0.063 9**	Vol_{t-3}	0.000 0	0.000 0	-0.001 7	-0.000 2	-0.000 1
VR_{t-4}	0.008 3	0.009 3	0.008 5	0.008 4	0.001 3	Vol_{t-4}	0.000 0	-0.000 3	0.001 3	-0.000 1	-0.000 1
VR_{t-5}	0.003 9	0.004 9	0.004 1	0.003 9	0.008 9	Vol_{t-5}	0.000 1	-0.004 4	0.000 6	-0.000 1	-0.000 1
VR_{t-6}	0.015 7***	0.016 3***	0.015 7***	0.015 7**	0.014 7**	Vol_{t-6}	0.000 0	0.000 8	-0.005 6	0.000 0	-0.000 1
VR_{t-7}	0.015 8***	0.016 8***	0.016 0***	0.015 9***	0.004 7	Vol_{t-7}	0.000 1	-0.004 4	0.007 9	0.000 0	-0.000 1
VR_{t-8}	0.000 0	0.000 8	0.000 3	-0.000 2	-0.001 809*	Vol_{t-8}	0.000 1	-0.013 5***	-0.007 2	0.000 0	-0.000 1
VR_{t-9}	-0.000 5	-0.000 3	-0.000 4	-0.000 5	0.012 8	Vol_{t-9}	0.000 1	-0.000 1	-0.011 6**	0.000 0	-0.000 1
VR_{t-10}	0.049 8***	0.053 3***	0.050 4***	0.049 5***	0.006 6	Vol_{t-10}	0.000 1	0.000 9	0.008 3	0.000 0	-0.000 1

***, ** and * stand for the significant level of 1%, 5%, and 10% respectively.

Table 5-14 Results for VAR Analysis of Put Options of Different Moneyness

	Dependent Variable: VR_t						Dependent Variable: VOL_t				
	Deep OTM	OTM	ATM	ITM	Deep ITM		Deep OTM	OTM	ATM	ITM	Deep ITM
Vol_{t-1}	0.000 0	0.000 0	0.000 0	0.000 0	0.000 0	VR_{t-1}	1.18E+08	1.40E+08***	-111 165.700 0	7 323.516 0	7 434.604 0
Vol_{t-2}	0.000 0	0.000 0	0.000 0	0.000 0	0.000 0	VR_{t-2}	-62 528 483.000 0	-85 702 213***	-25 919.180 0	-2 152.880 0	7 615.516 0
Vol_{t-3}	6.92E-13***	0.000 0	0.000 0	0.000 0	0.000 0	VR_{t-3}	-45 695 434.000 0	-33 298 326.000 0	-40 729.900 0	-2 908.841 0	-35 748.840 0
Vol_{t-4}	0.000 0	0.000 0	0.000 0	0.000 0	0.000 0	VR_{t-4}	2 328 889.000 0	23 545 931.000 0	75 335.460 0	-2 878.578 0	-17 219.620 0
Vol_{t-5}	0.000 0	0.000 0	0.000 0	0.000 0	0.000 0	VR_{t-5}	-22 474 928.000 0	-2 637 011.000 0	-81 579.340 0	8 576.165 0	20 077.090 0
Vol_{t-6}	0.000 0	0.000 0	0.000 0	0.000 0	0.000 0	VR_{t-6}	9 598 744.000 0	-17 774 737.000 0	9 519.783 0	-738.886 7	206 876.8**
Vol_{t-7}	0.000 0	0.000 0	0.000 0	0.000 0	0.000 0	VR_{t-7}	-32 258 069.000 0	-5 001 532.000 0	-59 832.180 0	-239.866 1	-156 317.800 0
Vol_{t-8}	6.10E-13***	0.000 0	8.00E-10***	0.000 0	0.000 0	VR_{t-8}	1.14E+08	-757 400.700 0	-323.297 0	-4 095.250 0	-4 625.035 0
Vol_{t-9}	1.25E-12***	0.000 0	8.24E-10***	0.000 0	0.000 0	VR_{t-9}	8 640 234.000 0	1 181 034.000 0	67 920.590 0	5 775.732 0	53 299.620 0
Vol_{t-10}	4.15E-12***	2.89E-12***	-5.99E-10***	5.25E-09**	0.000 0	VR_{t-10}	-55 327 977.000 0	433 688.900 0	-91 566.970 0	-3 777.672 0	-67 018.400 0

Table 5-14 (continued)

	Dependent Variable: VR_t						Dependent Variable: VOL_t				
	Deep OTM	OTM	ATM	ITM	Deep ITM		Deep OTM	OTM	ATM	ITM	Deep ITM
VR_{t-1}	0.782 8***	0.785 4***	0.785 1***	0.784 5***	0.814 6***	Vol_{t-1}	-0.000 2	-0.000 4	0.401 4***	0.186 7***	0.000 7
VR_{t-2}	0.042 3***	0.041 4***	0.041 4***	0.041 4***	0.034 0***	Vol_{t-2}	-0.000 2	0.000 0	0.123 8***	0.099 4***	0.000 7
VR_{t-3}	-0.048 8***	-0.049 3***	-0.049 4***	-0.049 3***	-0.063 8***	Vol_{t-3}	-0.000 1	-0.000 1	0.120 9***	0.086 2***	0.000 5
VR_{t-4}	0.008 6	0.008 4	0.008 3	0.008 3	0.001 3	Vol_{t-4}	-0.000 2	0.000 0	0.081 7***	0.072 6***	0.000 5
VR_{t-5}	0.003 9	0.003 9	0.003 9	0.003 9	0.008 9	Vol_{t-5}	-0.000 1	0.000 0	0.034 0***	0.067 1***	0.000 5
VR_{t-6}	0.015 5***	0.015 7***	0.015 7***	0.015 7***	0.014 7***	Vol_{t-6}	-0.000 1	0.000 1	0.038 8***	0.051 5***	0.000 5
VR_{t-7}	0.014 9***	0.015 9***	0.015 8***	0.015 8***	0.004 7	Vol_{t-7}	-0.000 1	0.000 1	0.025 6***	0.042 8***	0.000 5
VR_{t-8}	0.001 0	-0.000 2	-0.000 1	-0.000 1	-0.001 8	Vol_{t-8}	-0.000 2	0.000 0	0.023 9***	0.052 3***	0.000 4
VR_{t-9}	-0.000 7	-0.000 5	-0.000 6	-0.000 6	0.012 8	Vol_{t-9}	-0.000 3	0.000 0	0.028 9***	0.040 0***	0.000 4
VR_{t-10}	0.049 7***	0.049 5***	0.049 7***	0.049 7***	0.006 5	Vol_{t-10}	-0.000 3	-0.000 1	0.048 9***	0.032 5***	0.000 4

***, ** and * stand for the significant level of 1%, 5%, and 10% respectively.

Table 5-14 shows the result for VAR analysis of put options of different moneyness. As seen in the Table 5 - 14, ATM options have the strongest predictive power for the volatility of KOSPI200 index. This result is consistent with the findings of many previous studies, such as Pan & Poteshman (2008). In addition, as shown in the Table 5-14, that the trading volume of deep OTM options is larger than other options in the KOSPI200 index options markets. Based on this fact, it is reasonable to conjecture that deep OTM should have stronger predictive power on the future volatility of the KOSPI200 index. As reported in the first column Table 5-14, the coefficients estimated from the deep OTM put options are significant, indicating the put options volumes of deep OTM continuously also have significant predictive ability with respect to the volatility of KOSPI200 index. This finding is identical to the speculation above. On the other hand, when the put options volume across options moneyness are used as the dependent variable, the volatility only leads OTM put options volumes at lag 1 and lag 2.

Table 5 - 15 shows the relations between the unexpected put options volume of various options moneyness and the volatility of KOSPI200 index. First, the parameters and the statistical significance of VAR model in the Table 5-15 are slightly higher than the same those in the Table 5-14, which suggests that the information content of the unexpected put options volume is stronger than that of overall put options volume. When the volatility of spot index is used as the dependent variable, this study finds that the predictive power of the unexpected put options for the volatility of spot index is strongest for ATM options, less strong but still appreciable for deep OTM options, and weaker but still significant for ITM options. This finding is supported by Pan & Poteshman(2008), who argue that directional informed traders are fond of deep OTM options because of lower premium and higher leverage, while ATM is preferred by the volatility informed trader in view of high sensitivity to volatility. Such a result for in-the-money options is also possible because the informed traders are able to successfully hide their real trading in the aggregate trading of such options. But, in fact, informed traders appear to find near-the-money and out-of-the-money options as useful avenues for their trading activities. Such a trading strategy would likely blur the net effects on options price and trading volume that can be attributed to one particular group of informed traders. On the other hand, using the unexpected put options volumes as the dependent variable in VAR analysis, there is no significant relation between the unexpected put options volume and the volatility of the KOSPI200 index except OTM options. This result indicates that there is transient feedback relation between the volatility of KOSPI200 index and volume for OTM put options.

As shown in the Table 5-16, when the volatility of the spot index are used as dependent variable, this study finds only the put-call ratio of ATM has significant effect on the volatility of spot index. To the extent that the variation in the unexpected put-call ratio of ATM options can be seen as a leading indicator for the fluctuations of the volatility, it can help investors set investment strategy in advance. On the contrary, the lag volatility terms have significant effect on the put-call ratio of deep ITM options at lag 1, lag 2, lag 6 and lag 9.

Table 5-15　Results for VAR Analysis of Unexpected Put Options of Different Moneyness

Dependent Variable: VR_t						Dependent Variable: VOL_t					
	Deep OTM	OTM	ATM	ITM	Deep ITM		Deep OTM	OTM	ATM	ITM	Deep ITM
Vol_{t-1}	0.000 0	0.000 0	0.000 0	0.000 0	0.000 0	VR_{t-1}	1.2E+08	1.37E+08 ***	-70 443.360 0	7 934.766 0	6 860.377 0
Vol_{t-2}	0.000 0	0.000 0	0.000 0	0.000 0	0.000 0	VR_{t-2}	-61 798 887.000 0	-86 539 193 **	-61 699.300 0	-3 629.043 0	6 751.544 0
Vol_{t-3}	6.97E-13 ***	0.000 0	0.000 0	0.000 0	0.000 0	VR_{t-3}	-45 094 330.000 0	-34 012 944.000 0	-45 470.190 0	-3 395.899 0	-35 780.920 0
Vol_{t-4}	0.000 0	0.000 0	0.000 0	0.000 0	0.000 0	VR_{t-4}	3 064 300.000 0	22 616 412.000 0	85 385.130 0	-4 326.582 0	-16 424.810 0
Vol_{t-5}	0.000 0	0.000 0	0.000 0	0.000 0	0.000 0	VR_{t-5}	-21 738 717.000 0	-3 587 678.000 0	-90 878.950 0	7 313.508 0	21 105.170 0
Vol_{t-6}	0.000 0	0.000 0	0.000 0	0.000 0	0.000 0	VR_{t-6}	10 336 594.000 0	-18 724 993.000 0	19 337.800 0	-1 721.627 0	207 412.8 **
Vol_{t-7}	0.000 0	0.000 0	0.000 0	1.31E-09	0.000 0	VR_{t-7}	-31 539 598.000 0	-5 932 802.000 0	-58 482.040 0	-513.578 1	-156 654.300 0
Vol_{t-8}	6.15E-13 ***	0.000 0	6.28E-10 ***	5.63E-09 **	0.000 0	VR_{t-8}	1.15E+08.000 0	-1 473 921.000 0	-10 522.590 0	-4 662.739 0	-5 685.388 0
Vol_{t-9}	1.25E-12 ***	0.000 0	1.48E-09 ***	6.29E-09 ***	0.000 0	VR_{t-9}	9 297 610.000 0	324 545.700 0	64 272.800 0	5 359.948 0	52 374.310 0
Vol_{t-10}	4.16E-12 ***	2.80E-12 ***	1.23E-09 ***	8.37E-09 ***	0.000 0	VR_{t-10}	-52 700 690.000 0	-2 977 379.000 0	-100 452.000 0	-5 418.946 0	-66 025.920 0

Table 5-15（continued）

	Dependent Variable: VR_t						Dependent Variable: VOL_t				
	Deep OTM	OTM	ATM	ITM	Deep ITM		Deep OTM	OTM	ATM	ITM	Deep ITM
VR_{t-1}	0.782 8***	0.785 4***	0.784 5***	0.784 7***	0.814 6***	Vol_{t-1}	-0.000 1	-0.000 5	-0.003 0	0.000 3	0.000 0
VR_{t-2}	0.042 3***	0.041 4***	0.041 7***	0.041 5***	0.034 0***	Vol_{t-2}	0.000 0	0.000 0	0.010 1**	-0.000 4	0.000 0
VR_{t-3}	-0.048 8***	-0.049 3***	-0.049 2***	-0.049***	-0.063 8***	Vol_{t-3}	0.000 1	-0.000 2	-0.010 1**	-0.001 5	0.000 0
VR_{t-4}	0.008 6	0.008 4	0.008 4	0.008 4	0.001 3	Vol_{t-4}	0.000 0	-0.000 1	-0.004 8	0.005 3	0.000 0
VR_{t-5}	0.003 9	0.003 9	0.004 1	0.004 0	0.008 9	Vol_{t-5}	0.000 1	-0.000 1	0.000 4	-0.004 9	0.000 0
VR_{t-6}	0.015 4***	0.015 7***	0.015 8***	0.015 8***	0.014 7**	Vol_{t-6}	0.000 1	0.000 0	0.005 0	0.003 1	0.000 1
VR_{t-7}	0.014 9**	0.015 9***	0.015 9***	0.015 9***	0.004 7	Vol_{t-7}	0.000 1	0.000 0	0.001 2	-0.002 1	0.000 1
VR_{t-8}	0.001 0	-0.000 2	0.000 1	0.000 0	-0.001 8	Vol_{t-8}	0.000 1	0.000 0	-0.007 0	-0.000 4	0.000 1
VR_{t-9}	-0.000 7	-0.000 5	-0.000 5	-0.000 5	0.012 8*	Vol_{t-9}	0.000 0	-0.000 1	-0.006 6	-0.009 0*	0.000 1
VR_{t-10}	0.049 7	0.049 5***	0.050 1***	0.049 7***	0.006 5	Vol_{t-10}	0.000 0	-0.000 1	-0.002 8	0.010 0*	-0.000 1

***, ** and * stand for the significant level of 1%, 5%, and 10% respectively.

Table 5-16　Results for VAR Analysis of Put-Call Ratio of Different Moneyness

Dependent Variable: VR_t						Dependent Variable: PC_t					
	Deep OTM	OTM	ATM	ITM	Deep ITM		Deep OTM	OTM	ATM	ITM	Deep ITM
PC_{t-1}	0.000 0	0.000 0	-0.000 1	0.000 0	0.000 0	VR_{t-1}	-1.164 1	0.719 7	0.117 2	-0.299 8	-3.972 4**
PC_{t-2}	0.000 0	0.000 0	0.000 1	0.000 0	0.000 0	VR_{t-2}	-0.172 2	-0.340 3	0.628 1	1.271 3	6.869 4***
PC_{t-3}	0.000 0	0.000 0	0.000 0	0.000 0	0.000 0	VR_{t-3}	0.497 0	-0.161 2	-0.515 1	0.581 1	-3.907 9*
PC_{t-4}	-0.000 1	0.000 1	0.000 0	0.000 0	0.000 0	VR_{t-4}	0.177 3	-0.112 7	0.276 8	-0.714 5	-0.266 9
PC_{t-5}	0.000 0	0.000 1	0.000 1*	0.000 0	0.000 0	VR_{t-5}	-0.382 2	0.280 7	-0.990 3	0.844 3	2.894 7
PC_{t-6}	0.000 0	0.000 0	0.000 1**	0.000 0	0.000 0	VR_{t-6}	-0.094 4	-0.159 0	1.034 553*	-0.665 3	-4.688 2**
PC_{t-7}	0.000 0	0.000 0	0.000 1	5.31E-05*	0.000 0	VR_{t-7}	0.065 0	0.255 7	0.556 7	0.033 9	3.284 4
PC_{t-8}	0.000 0	0.000 0	0.000 0	0.000 0	0.000 0	VR_{t-8}	0.021 5	-0.330 0	-0.847 2	0.179 8	-1.963 6
PC_{t-9}	-0.000 1	0.000 0	0.000 1**	0.000 0	3.24E-05*	VR_{t-9}	-1.147 2	0.422 4	-0.052 3	-0.001 8	5.784 2***
PC_{t-10}	-0.000 2***	-0.000 2	-0.000 4***	0.000 0	0.000 0	VR_{t-10}	-0.230 1	0.325 5	0.283 6	-0.947 1	-1.843 6

Table 5-16 (continued)

	Dependent Variable: VR_t					Dependent Variable: PC_t				
	Deep OTM	OTM	ATM	ITM	Deep ITM		Deep OTM	OTM	ATM	ITM	Deep ITM
VR_{t-1}	0.780 7***	0.785 2***	0.784 7***	0.785 0***	0.814 4***	PC_{t-1}	0.379 0***	0.436 8***	0.465 8***	0.351 6***	0.277 9***
VR_{t-2}	0.040 5***	0.041 3***	0.041 2***	0.041 4***	0.034 0***	PC_{t-2}	0.112 5***	0.148 2***	0.196 3***	0.159 4***	0.130 4***
VR_{t-3}	-0.050 1***	-0.049 3***	-0.049 1***	-0.049 4***	-0.063 9***	PC_{t-3}	0.090 3***	0.105 3***	0.102 9***	0.108 3***	0.099 6***
VR_{t-4}	0.007 2	0.008 4	0.008 4	0.008 3	0.001 4	PC_{t-4}	0.065 1***	0.063 0***	0.068 1***	0.073 1***	0.081 2***
VR_{t-5}	0.002 8	0.003 9	0.004 0	0.003 9	0.009 0	PC_{t-5}	0.067 1***	0.078 7***	0.047 5***	0.056 1***	0.055 1***
VR_{t-6}	0.014 6**	0.015 7***	0.015 6***	0.015 6***	0.014 5**	PC_{t-6}	0.057 3***	0.028 9***	0.023 1***	0.048 2***	0.055 7***
VR_{t-7}	0.014 9**	0.015 7***	0.015 6***	0.015 8***	0.004 7	PC_{t-7}	0.036 6***	0.022 4***	0.018 5***	0.035 4***	0.043 1***
VR_{t-8}	-0.000 8	-0.000 1	0.000 1	0.000 0	-0.001 7	PC_{t-8}	0.034 8***	0.019 4***	0.012 0***	0.035 5***	0.051 4***
VR_{t-9}	-0.001 7	-0.000 4	-0.000 9	-0.000 7	0.012 5	PC_{t-9}	0.034 3***	0.028 5***	0.016 5***	0.019 0***	0.049 0***
VR_{t-10}	0.046 1	0.049 6	0.049 7	0.049 6	0.006 6	PC_{t-10}	0.053 5***	0.011 0***	0.007 6	0.039 6***	0.061 5***

***, ** and * stand for the significant level of 1%, 5%, and 10% respectively.

Table 5-17 Results for VAR Analysis of Unexpected Put-Call Ratio of Different Moneyness

Dependent Variable: VR_t						Dependent Variable: PC_t					
	Deep OTM	OTM	ATM	ITM	Deep ITM		Deep OTM	OTM	ATM	ITM	Deep ITM
PC_{t-1}	-3.57E-05	3.28E-05	-4.92E-05	1.14E-05	7.46E-06	VR_{t-1}	-1.086 5	0.727 0	0.186 9	-0.371 7	-4.403 2***
PC_{t-2}	1.51E-05	2.01E-05	6.99E-05	-7.18E-06	3.23E-06	VR_{t-2}	-0.012 8	-0.320 9	0.679 7	1.259 3	6.525 6***
PC_{t-3}	2.46E-05	-1.82E-05	-1.97E-05	-1.76E-05	8.31E-06	VR_{t-3}	0.621 2	-0.143 6	-0.508 0	0.577 8	-3.922 2*
PC_{t-4}	-5.05E-05	5.14E-05	3.40E-05	1.47E-05	1.71E-05	VR_{t-4}	0.331 3	-0.095 8	0.300 1	-0.730 4	-0.330 7
PC_{t-5}	-3.60E-05	6.31E-05	0.000 1**	-1.21E-05	-1.84E-05	VR_{t-5}	-0.296 8	0.313 9	-0.981 6	0.829 5	2.906 4
PC_{t-6}	-2.90E-05	5.95E-05	0.000 2***	-2.43E-06	-3.27E-05*	VR_{t-6}	0.071 0	-0.160 8	1.050 7*	-0.689 5	-4.517*
PC_{t-7}	-3.82E-05	5.25E-05	0.000 2***	4.41E-05	-7.94E-06	VR_{t-7}	0.270 3	0.241 9	0.590 6	0.005 7	3.141 2
PC_{t-8}	-7.73E-05**	-3.79E-05	6.16E-05**	2.06E-05	-2.93E-05	VR_{t-8}	0.126 6	-0.303 1	-0.880 6	0.149 2	-2.029 2
PC_{t-9}	-9.96E-05***	-4.67E-07	0.000 2***	6.64E-06	1.48E-05	VR_{t-9}	-1.088 7	0.450 1	-0.001 1	0.018 5	5.669 5***
PC_{t-10}	-0.000 2***	-0.000 3***	-0.000 4***	-2.42E-05	-3.00E-06	VR_{t-10}	0.316 0	0.364 4	0.297 3	-0.992 8	-1.952 3

Table 5-17 (continued)

Dependent Variable: VR_t						Dependent Variable: PC_t					
	Deep OTM	OTM	ATM	ITM	Deep ITM		Deep OTM	OTM	ATM	ITM	Deep ITM
VR_{t-1}	0.784 6***	0.785 3***	0.785 3***	0.785 3***	0.814 5***	PC_{t-1}	0.000 5	0.000 0	-0.000 1	0.000 0	0.002 0
VR_{t-2}	0.041 5***	0.041 3***	0.041 2***	0.041 5***	0.034 0***	PC_{t-2}	-0.002 3	0.000 0	-0.000 3	-0.000 1	-0.004 9
VR_{t-3}	-0.049 2***	-0.049 1***	-0.048 9***	-0.049 3***	-0.063 8***	PC_{t-3}	0.002 0	0.000 2	0.001 0	-0.000 6	-0.000 5
VR_{t-4}	0.008 3	0.008 5	0.008 5	0.008 3	0.001 4	PC_{t-4}	0.001 6	0.000 1	0.001 6	-0.000 9	0.001 9
VR_{t-5}	0.003 9	0.003 9	0.004 0	0.004 0	0.009 0	PC_{t-5}	-0.003 3	-0.001 0	-0.003 8	0.001 8	0.000 6
VR_{t-6}	0.015 7***	0.015 7***	0.015 5***	0.015 7***	0.014 6**	PC_{t-6}	0.005 3	-0.001 2	-0.003 2	0.004 7	0.008 7
VR_{t-7}	0.016 0***	0.015 7***	0.015 6***	0.015 8***	0.004 7	PC_{t-7}	-0.004 4	-0.002 0	0.000 0	0.003 6	-0.003 6
VR_{t-8}	-0.000 1	0.000 0	0.000 2	0.000 0	-0.001 7	PC_{t-8}	0.000 6	-0.001 2	-0.000 6	-0.000 9	0.005 9
VR_{t-9}	-0.000 8	-0.000 4	-0.001 0	-0.000 6	0.012 5*	PC_{t-9}	-0.001 0	0.000 0	0.002 7	-0.005 4	0.007 8
VR_{t-10}	0.049 9	0.049 7***	0.050 0	0.049 8***	0.006 7	PC_{t-10}	0.008 0	-0.000 7	-0.001 3	0.003 0	0.004 5

***, ** and * stand for the significant level of 1%, 5%, and 10% respectively.

Table 5 - 17 shows the relations between unexpected put-call ratio of different moneyness and the volatility of KOSPI200 index. Firstly, when the volatility of the KOSPI200 index is used as dependent variable in VAR analysis, this study finds that the coefficients estimators for the influence of unexpected put-call ratio of ATM options on the volatility are significant from lag 5 to lag 10, coupled with the weaker but significant effect for deep OTM options. It is obviously that the influence of unexpected put-call ratio on the volatility is much stronger than put-call ratio. These results not only provide distinct evidence on the existence of volatility informed trading, but also underline the information content of ATM and deep OTM options for the volatility of KOSPI200 index. On the other hand, the lag volatility term also has significant influence on the unexpected put-call ratio of deep ITM at lag 1, 2, 9.

5.4 Robustness Test

The VAR model specifies that each endogenous variable depends upon its own lagged values and the lagged values of the other endogenous variables involved. However, the VAR model omits the contemporaneous interaction among the variables, and thus ignores the possibility that the variables may be simultaneously determined. Koch (1993) argues that if the variables in question are structurally related within the same time interval, then the VAR-based parameters yield biased and inconsistent estimates of the structural dynamic linkages. He advocates the estimation of the parameters in the context of a simultaneous equations model. Following Koch (1993), the Granger causality test is also used to estimate the relation between unexpected options volume and the volatility of KOSPI200 index.

The Granger causality test is a statistical hypothesis test for determining whether one time series is useful in forecasting another. The null hypothesis is that the y does not Granger Cause x. A user specifies the two time series, x and y, along with the significance level and the maximum number of lags to be considered. The function chooses the optimal lag length for x and y based on the Bayesian Information Criterion. The function produces the F-statistic for the Granger Causality Test along with the corresponding critical value. The null hypothesis that y does not Granger Cause x is rejected if the F-statistic is greater than the critical value. According to Granger causality, if a signal X "Granger-causes" a signal Y, then past values of X should contain information that helps predict Y above and beyond the information contained in past values of Y alone.

5.4.1 The Informational Role of Various Investors

A Granger-causality analysis has been carried out in order to assess whether there is any potential predictability power of one indicator for the other. The empirical results presented in this paper are calculated within a simple Granger-causality test in order to test whether the unexpected options volumes "Granger cause" the volatility of KOSPI200 index and vice versa.

Table 5-18 indicates the results for Granger Causality of the unexpected call options volumes of various investor classifications and the volatility of

KOSPI200 index. The values of F-statistic suggest that the unexpected call options volumes of foreign investors, individual investors and institutional investors Granger-causes the volatility of KOSPI200 index respectively. On the other hand, the volatility of KOSPI200 index Granger-cause the unexpected call options volumes of every investor classification separately. Therefore, the results demonstrate that there are feed–back relation between past values of the unexpected call options volumes of various investors' classification and the volatility of KOSPI200 index.

Table 5–18 Results for Granger Causality Test of Unexpected Call Options Volume of Various Investors

	Null Hypothesis	F-statistic	P-value
Individual investor	VOL Does not Granger Cause VR	156. 895 0	0. 000 0
	VR Does not Granger Cause VOL	2. 900 5	0. 001 2
Foreign investor	VOL Does not Granger Cause VR	82. 699 4	0. 000 0
	VR Does not Granger Cause VOL	7. 759 6	0. 000 0
Institutional investor	VOL Does not Granger Cause VR	48. 955 7	0. 000 0
	VR Does not Granger Cause VOL	7. 358 1	0. 000 0

The findings are the same as the results of Table 5 – 19. Table 5 – 19 indicates the results for Granger Causality of the unexpected put options volumes of various investor classifications and the volatility of KOSPI200 index. As seen in the Table 5 – 19, the unexpected put options volumes of various investor classifications are useful in predicting the volatility of the KOSPI200 index; similarly, there is predictive power of the volatility of the KOSPI200 index for the unexpected put options volume for various investors.

As expected from the above results, this study finds that the results of Granger causality test strengthen the findings of the above VAR analysis.

Table 5-19 Results for Granger Causality Test of Unexpected Put Options Volume of Various Investors

	Null Hypothesis	F-statistic	P-value
Individual investor	VOL Does not Granger Cause VR	72. 473 0	0. 000 0
	VR Does not Granger Cause VOL	9. 103 5	0. 000 0
Foreign investor	VOL Does not Granger Cause VR	135. 920 0	0. 000 0
	VR Does not Granger Cause VOL	11. 784 7	0. 000 0
Institutional investor	VOL Does not Granger Cause VR	27. 093 2	0. 000 0
	VR Does not Granger Cause VOL	6. 277 7	0. 000 0

Table 5-20 indicates the results for Granger Causality of the unexpected put-call ratios of various investors and the volatility of KOSPI200 index. The result demonstrates that past values of the unexpected put-call ratios of every investor classification in this research do not contribute to the prediction of the present value of the volatility of KOSPI200 index even with past values of the volatility of KOSPI200 index. Likewise, this study finds that the volatility of the index does not Granger-cause the unexpected put-call ratios of any investor classification, according to the F-statistic. This result is somewhat surprising, which is attributed to the put-call ratio is a valid measurement indicator for directional informed trading, but not a touchstone for the volatility informed trader.

Table 5-20 Results for Granger Causality Test of Unexpected Put-Call Ratio of Various Investors

	Null Hypothesis	F-statistic	P-value
Individual investor	VOL Does not Granger Cause VR	0. 774 3	0. 653 9
	VR Does not Granger Cause VOL	0. 501 9	0. 889 9
Foreign investor	VOL Does not Granger Cause VR	1. 259 1	0. 247 5
	VR Does not Granger Cause VOL	0. 814 5	0. 614 7
Institutional investor	VOL Does not Granger Cause VR	1. 524 7	0. 123 4
	VR Does not Granger Cause VOL	0. 642 2	0. 778 6

5. 4. 2 The Information Content of Options Moneyness

The results of Granger Causality for the unexpected call options volumes of different degree of options moneyness are represented in Table 5-21. The values of F-statistic suggest that the unexpected call options volumes of OTM and ATM options Granger-causes the volatility of KOSPI200 index. On the other hand, the volatility of KOSPI200 index does not cause the unexpected call options volumes except ATM and OTM options. Thus, it can be argued that there are feed-back relationship between the unexpected call options volume for ATM and OTM options and the volatility.

The results of Granger Causality test for the unexpected put options volumes of different degree of options moneyness and the volatility of KOSPI200 index are reported in the Table 5-22. For ATM options, the values of F-statistic suggest that the unexpected put options volumes of ATM Granger-causes the volatility of KOSPI200 index, and the volatility of KOSPI200 index Granger-cause the unexpected put options volumes of ATM. There is feedback relationship between the unexpected put options of ATM and the volatility of KOSPI200 index. For deep OTM options, the values of F-statistic suggest that the unexpected put options volumes of deep OTM options Granger-causes the volatility of KOSPI200 index, while the volatility of KOSPI200 index does not cause the unexpected put options volumes of deep OTM options. Thus, it can be argued that past values of the unexpected put options volumes of deep OTM options contribute to the prediction of the present value of the volatility of KOSPI200 index even with past values of the volatility of KOSPI200 index. Conversely, the associated F-statistics of OTM, ITM and deep ITM give the opposite results. There seem to be no Granger-Causality between the volatility and the unexpected put options volumes, because the F-statistics are insignificant. In short, the results of Granger causality test are approximately in agreement with the finding of VAR model, which again reinforces the existence of informed trading.

Table 5-21 Results for Granger Causality Test of Unexpected Volume of Call Options of Different Moneyness

	Null Hypothesis	F-statistic	P-value
Deep OTM options	VOL Does not Granger Cause VR	0. 154 7	0. 998 8
	VR Does not Granger Cause VOL	0. 132 7	0. 999 4
OTM options	VOL Does not Granger Cause VR	26. 161 7	0. 000 0
	VR Does not Granger Cause VOL	8. 254 7	0. 000 0
ATM options	VOL Does not Granger Cause VR	7. 270 6	0. 000 0
	VR Does not Granger Cause VOL	2. 489 2	0. 005 6
ITM options	VOL Does not Granger Cause VR	0. 796 8	0. 632 0
	VR Does not Granger Cause VOL	0. 179 2	0. 997 7
Deep ITM Options	VOL Does not Granger Cause VR	0. 842 0	0. 587 9
	VR Does not Granger Cause VOL	0. 068 4	1. 000 0

The results of Granger Causality for the unexpected put-call ratios across moneyness are represented in Table 5−23. The result is similar as in the Table 5−22. For ATM and deep OTM options, their values of F-statistic suggest that the unexpected put-call ratios Granger-cause the volatility of KOSPI200 index respectively. On the other hand, the volatility of KOSPI200 index does not cause the unexpected put-call ratios of ATM and deep OTM options. Thus, it can be argued that past values of the unexpected put-call ratios are useful in forecasting the future volatility of KOSPI200 index. Besides, the associated F-statistics of OTM and ITM options give the opposite results. There seem to be no Granger−Causality between the volatility and the unexpected put-call ratios. In addition, the volatility of KOSPI200 index has Granger-causality on the unexpected put-call ratio of deep ITM options.

Table 5−22 Results for Granger Causality Test of Unexpected Volume of Put Option of Different Moneyness

	Null Hypothesis	F-statistic	P-value
Deep OTM options	VOL Does not Granger Cause VR	4. 129 8	0. 000 0
	VR Does not Granger Cause VOL	0. 233 1	0. 993 1
OTM options	VOL Does not Granger Cause VR	0. 793 7	0. 635 0
	VR Does not Granger Cause VOL	0. 160 9	0. 998 6
ATM options	VOL Does not Granger Cause VR	2. 836 6	0. 001 6
	VR Does not Granger Cause VOL	2. 363 0	0. 008 7
ITM options	VOL Does not Granger Cause VR	0. 178 8	0. 997 7
	VR Does not Granger Cause VOL	0. 795 3	0. 633 4
Deep ITM Options	VOL Does not Granger Cause VR	0. 178 8	0. 997 7
	VR Does not Granger Cause VOL	0. 795 3	0. 633 4

Table 5-23 Results for Granger Causality Test of Unexpected Put-Call Ratio of Different Moneyness

	Null Hypothesis	F-statistic	P-value
Deep OTM options	VOL Does not Granger Cause VR	1. 761 0	0. 061 9
	VR Does not Granger Cause VOL	0. 863 3	0. 567 2
OTM options	VOL Does not Granger Cause VR	0. 774 5	0. 653 7
	VR Does not Granger Cause VOL	0. 943 5	0. 491 4
ATM options	VOL Does not Granger Cause VR	3. 065 9	0. 000 7
	VR Does not Granger Cause VOL	1. 510 0	0. 128 5
ITM options	VOL Does not Granger Cause VR	0. 394 8	0. 949 7
	VR Does not Granger Cause VOL	0. 980 4	0. 457 9
Deep ITM Options	VOL Does not Granger Cause VR	1. 263 4	0. 244 9
	VR Does not Granger Cause VOL	2. 097 1	0. 021 3

5. 5 The Response of Unexpected Options Volumes to News Announcements

5. 5. 1 The Response of Unexpected Options Volume of Various Investors to News Announcements

Although it is very unlikely that anyone might possess private information about the market index in a fairly large and efficient equity market, as argued by Richards (2005), foreign capital flows in the emerging markets are so large that they create price pressure. This clearly offers profitable opportunity for investors who have access to the information. In order to analyze the informational role of various investors in Korean security market, this research relates the unexpected options volume of various investors to the news announcement. It is assumed that if informed trader should have private information on the future movement of market in advance of news announcements, they must use options trading to maximize their profits. So it is necessary to track the change of the options volume before news announcement to verify the information role of various investors, based on the fact that the informed trading is sensitive to news announcement in advance.

Table 5-24 and Table 5-25 demonstrate the reactions of the unexpected call and put options volume for various investors to news announcements respectively. The result in Table 5-24 is generally in line with Table 5-25. Most of the unexpected volumes of foreign investors make significantly strong and quick reaction to the news in advance. In addition, the reaction of the unexpected volume of foreign investors to news announcement is obviously stronger than individual investors and institutional investors according to the value of F-statistic. This result is consistent with the finding of Chang, Hsei & Lai (2009), who argue that foreign investors as informed trader in emerging market have significant predictive power on the return of underlying asset, just like the big fish in the small pond. Conversely, individual investors who account for a considerable portion of options market trading volume, make no strong response to the good or bad news in advance of announcements. This result indicates that individual investors have less information on market movement than foreign investors and institutional investors. This result is consistent with the finding of Kim & Lee (2010), who give a rational explanation that individual investors engage in speculative trading in the expectation of " winning the lottery" , not because of informed trading. As reported in the Table 5-24 and 5-25, the reaction of the unexpected call options volume for institutional investors to news announcements is also significant, although the response is not stronger than foreign investors. It is noteworthy that the reaction of unexpected volume of call options is not quicker and stronger than the reaction of unexpected volume of put options according to the F-statistic. In summary, the results in Table 5-24 and Table 5-25 not only demonstrate the existence of informed trading, but also different sensitivity to the news announcement further verify that influence of foreign investors and institutional investors on the future volatility of underlying asset accounts for the informed trading.

The reaction of the unexpected put-call ratio for various investors to news announcements is reported in Table 5-26. Regardless of good news and bad news, the reaction of the unexpected put-call ratio for foreign investors is obviously stronger than individual investors and institutional investors according to the value of F-statistic. This result is consistent with the finding in the table 5-24 and table 5-25, which again verify the superior predictability of foreign investors.

Table 5-24 The Response of Unexpected Call Options Volume of Various Investors to News Announcements

	Good News Event			Bad News Event		
	Individual investor	Foreign investor	Institutional investor	Individual investor	Foreign investor	Institutional investor
Constant	-160. 404 4	-25. 099 8	-162. 974 4	-94. 427 3	-40. 162 4	-160. 966 3
Return	-81 626. 870 0	-9 958. 450 0	-44 061. 190 0	-103 955. 200 0	-26 548. 190 0	-89 995. 970 0
t=-12	-1 164. 527 0	-4 664. 620 0**	-11 105. 790 0**	-290. 020 9	-3 411. 746 0***	-7 679. 880 0***
t=-11	-3 567. 133 0	-19 063. 430 0***	-25 820. 370 0***	-8 447. 264 0***	-20 071. 380 0***	-23 405. 780 0***
t=-10	-2 629. 314 0	-2 377. 268 0*	-10 245. 520 00***	3 077. 581 0	315. 417 2	5 714. 316 0*
t=-9	51 164. 040 0***	31 909. 060 0***	62 336. 860 0***	23 933. 730 0***	17 032. 440 0***	25 771. 040 0***
t=-8	4 572. 513*	5 311. 114***	18 777. 790 0***	12 029. 360 0***	9 766. 689 0***	30 218. 880 0***
t=-7	4 109. 619 0	3 825. 543 00***	18 379. 930 0***	2 050. 190 0	2 771. 178 0**	6 564. 477 0**
t=-6	2 318. 644 0	3 108. 268 00**	6 341. 882 0*	409. 978 0	783. 277 6	3 284. 896 0
t=-5	2 084. 668 0	963. 300 0	4 126. 875 0	1 495. 885 0	391. 373 1	602. 775 5
t=-4	682. 847 4	3 073. 800 0	9 134. 014**	2 305. 486 0	6 783. 225 0***	14 652. 440 0***
t=-3	98. 480 5	1 412. 131 0	8 044. 550 0	-7 376. 840 0**	-1 464. 505 0	16. 809 3
t=-2	636. 280 4	-1 414. 685 0	-248. 315 9	-4 260. 258 0	-1 069. 541 0	-936. 061 4
t=-1	-4 233. 042 0	-1 993. 801 0	-2 116. 701 0	-7 540. 797**	-2 438. 512 0	-8 943. 295 0
t=0	-3 493. 320 0	-2 094. 453 0	-8 487. 756 0	-283. 145 3	1 397. 051 0	2 363. 086 0

Table 5-24 (continued)

	Good News Event			Bad News Event		
	Individual investor	Foreign investor	Institutional investor	Individual investor	Foreign investor	Institutional investor
t=1	2 346. 325 0	-571. 611 5	-305. 228 9	-1 638. 517 0	-172. 816 2	4 528. 426 0
t=2	-1 631. 487 0	-46. 306 9	-2 799. 209 0	8 065. 774 0**	4 607. 021 0	6 138. 930 0
t=3	-4 720. 129 0	-2 077. 214 0	645. 557 4	-5 539. 888 0*	-2 882. 940 0	1 672. 650 0
t=4	-79. 410 5	-874. 248 1	768. 625 8	551. 264 0	1 232. 586 0	413. 601 2
t=5	-4 108. 438 0	-3 453. 197 0	-9 135. 169 0	-1 630. 364 0	-1 907. 234 0	-5 409. 351 0
t=6	-1 727. 247 0	-1 791. 827 0	-954. 091 5	-4 537. 717 0	-770. 878 3	-2 152. 044 0
t=7	-3 316. 164 0	-1 028. 589 0	-5 823. 916 0	281. 468 7	-705. 184 4	-2 698. 510 0
t=8	820. 233 0	2 279. 669 0	-2 360. 752 0	-351. 168 9	660. 744 7	-3 765. 608 0
t=9	-1 130. 259 0	-713. 954 1	-2 475. 219 0	-2 915. 088 0	-2 514. 667 0	-8 071. 476 0
t=10	-8 555. 586 0***	-10 454. 250 0**	-15 513. 710 0***	-5 673. 745 0*	-12 814. 820 0***	-13 611. 040 0**
t=11	-1 756. 346 0	-3 118. 025 0**	-3 294. 065 0	-1 990. 280 0	-1 762. 524 0	-7 087. 922 0
t=12	17 235. 990 0***	8 149. 740 0***	17 482. 930 0***	28 970. 330 0***	15 416. 560 0***	36 251. 10***
Adjusted R^2	0. 011 7	0. 021 6	0. 012 0	0. 007 3	0. 016 5	0. 007 4
F-statistic	17. 848 4	32. 433 0	18. 317 7	11. 503 8	24. 790 9	11. 530 2
Prob (F-statistic)	0. 000 0	0. 000 0	0. 000 0	0. 000 0	0. 000 0	0. 000 0

***, ** and * stand for the significant level of 1%, 5%, and 10% respectively.

Table 5-25 The Response of Unexpected Put Options Volume of Various Investors to News Announcements

	Good News Event			Bad News Event		
	Individual investor	Foreign investor	Institutional investor	Individual investor	Foreign investor	Institutional investor
Constant	-131.233 0	-57.192 1	-124.333 6	-74.476 1	-41.870 5	-57.337 0
Return	1 858.279 0	13 949.110 0	-66 303.310 0	-16 635.490 0	14 290.900 0	-69 828.560 0
t=-12	-1 592.886 0	-4 967.610 0***	-3 568.218 0	-75.800 3	-1 489.190 0	-4 827.016**
t=-11	-4 490.271 0***	-16 109.480 0***	-14 183.590 0***	-11 731.590 0***	-16 679.440 0***	-17 570.650 0***
t=-10	-1 379.403 0	-3 327.494 0***	-2 391.833 0	95.024 1	18.696 2	-3 803.626 0**
t=-9	42 771.330***	29 597.010 0***	36 067.790 0***	20 199.360 0***	16 872.790 0***	13 906.880 0***
t=-8	7 803.334 0***	9 797.281 0***	15 821.640 0***	10 008.110 0***	12 605.430 0***	14 282.880 0***
t=-7	5 201.116 0**	7 801.317 0***	6 924.429 0**	2 090.265 0	3 042.787 0**	3 140.257 0
t=-6	642.508 4	4 155.870 0***	6 885.429 0**	2 666.840 0	4 380.293 0***	4 312.988 0**
t=-5	1 674.362 0	1 373.291 0	7 143.453 0***	-2 050.698 0	-1 060.794 0	-72.002 5
t=-4	482.297 2	2 180.229 0	4 065.968 0	1 376.872 0	3 735.270 0**	6 069.415 0**
t=-3	1 180.730 0	772.029 7	1 025.301 0	-1 786.704 0	-2 054.963 0	-1 002.599 0
t=-2	-694.352 3	-1 793.734 0	-3 615.527 0	721.042 8	-1 366.106 0	5 621.862 0*
t=-1	-3 229.030 0	-1 285.273 0	146.487 4	-4 990.597**	-1 078.649 0	-3 405.784 0
t=0	-3 966.324 0**	509.400 3	296.020 1	1 042.997 0	2 697.872 0	1 333.073 0

Table 5-25（continued）

	Good News Event			Bad News Event		
	Individual investor	Foreign investor	Institutional investor	Individual investor	Foreign investor	Institutional investor
t=1	-3 970. 172 0**	-3 006. 931 0	-3 264. 801 0	-548. 214 9	184. 632 8	1 372. 202 0
t=2	-1 765. 141 0	-523. 742 4	-4 731. 412**	2 992. 339 0	2 032. 988 0	4 531. 363 0
t=3	-3 247. 362 0	870. 176 0	-5 451. 529 0	-2 499. 557 0	-638. 007 0	-3 117. 358 0
t=4	-1 008. 317 0	1 246. 044 0	579. 445 1	1 119. 827 0	2 524. 718 0	-833. 824 2
t=5	-2 772. 778 0	-1 873. 636 0	-6 248. 602 0	-2 342. 830 0	-845. 009 2	-1 148. 138 0
t=6	-2 987. 609 0	-293. 829 6	-1 594. 400 0	-3 186. 922 0	613. 116 7	-3 483. 379 0
t=7	-1 730. 297 0	1 246. 408 0	799. 619 9	-964. 783 9	-342. 045 8	-2 293. 788 0
t=8	-1 000. 054 0	-1 125. 742 0	-1 517. 809 0	-1 171. 807 0	-2 290. 064 0	-4 772. 706 0
t=9	2 974. 443 0	-2 577. 651 0	-2 193. 373 0	-1 772. 991 0	-4 137. 130**	-5 050. 948 0
t=10	-7 007. 002 0***	-10 791. 370 0***	-10 605. 570 00***	-7 970. 778 0***	-14 313. 170 0***	-9 692. 583 0***
t=11	-3 912. 907 0**	-4 834. 653 0***	-3 242. 287 0	-250. 054 5	-2 051. 523 0	2 514. 771 0
t=12	18 275. 160 0***	8 467. 696 0***	17 223. 060 0***	23 762. 950 0***	12 230. 460 0***	23 762. 040 0***
Adjusted R^2	0. 014 2	0. 020 8	0. 009 2	0. 008 0	0. 015 5	0. 005 3
F-statistic	21. 412 6	31. 207 6	14. 238 4	12. 525 1	23. 361 8	8. 534 4
Prob(F-statistic)	0. 000 0	0. 000 0	0. 000 0	0. 000 0	0. 000 0	0. 000 0

***, ** and * stand for the significant level of 1%, 5%, and 10% respectively.

Table 5-26 The Response of Unexpected Put-Call Ratio of Various Investors to News Announcements

	Good News Event			Bad News Event		
	Individual investor	Foreign investor	Institutional investor	Individual investor	Foreign investor	Institutional investor
Constant	-0.000 1	0.000 0	-0.000 1	0.000 2	0.000 3	0.000 3
Return	0.120 9	0.072 9	-0.003 4	0.117 1	0.068 3	0.056 6
t=-12	-0.002 9	-0.013 818**	-0.005 4	-0.000 8	0.003 7	-0.000 1
t=-11	-0.008 4	0.014 7**	0.014 6	-0.025 2***	-0.020 6**	-0.025 9**
t=-10	-0.003 5	-0.059 4***	0.020 2**	-0.008 7*	-0.013 3**	-0.036 0***
t=-9	-0.002 3	-0.013 2*	-0.029 9***	0.004 0	-0.000 9	-0.001 7
t=-8	0.020 6***	0.016 7**	-0.005 0	0.000 1	-0.000 7	-0.016 1
t=-7	0.012 3*	0.008 4	-0.007 7	0.002 6	0.000 2	-0.007 4
t=-6	-0.000 9	0.007 6	0.004 6	0.008 6*	0.009 3	0.003 2
t=-5	0.011 3	0.009 8	0.005 7	-0.008 4	-0.002 4	-0.004 7
t=-4	0.004 9	0.003 8	0.012 6	-0.003 0	-0.000 8	-0.009 2
t=-3	-0.003 1	0.000 3	-0.010 7	0.003 7	0.005 7	-0.002 8
t=-2	0.002 3	0.005 7	0.000 1	0.002 1	-0.002 0	0.015 7
t=-1	0.003 9	0.002 6	0.008 2	0.001 8	0.000 9	0.001 7
t=0	-0.002 9	0.006 8	0.017 0	0.004 0	-0.004 7	-0.005 2

Table 5-26 (continued)

	Good News Event			Bad News Event		
	Individual investor	Foreign investor	Institutional investor	Individual investor	Foreign investor	Institutional investor
t=1	−0.005 5	−0.004 3	−0.014 5	−0.002 4	0.001 8	−0.013 3
t=2	−0.006 1	−0.001 7	−0.009 7	−0.013 8	−0.015 1	−0.007 8
t=3	−0.002 2	0.009 8	−0.011 5	0.004 0	−0.001 8	0.006 3
t=4	0.001 5	0.000 7	−0.007 3	0.001 3	−0.008 0	−0.013 5
t=5	0.004 8	0.003 2	0.004 4	−0.004 4	−0.005 4	−0.004 3
t=6	−0.009 1	0.000 0	−0.010 3	0.002 6	−0.000 4	0.003 2
t=7	0.010 927*	0.006 3	0.012 4	−0.006 4	−0.006 6	−0.005 4
t=8	−0.004 2	0.002 4	0.006 7	0.001 3	−0.002 7	−0.000 3
t=9	0.012 2**	0.002 6	−0.007 9	−0.004 9	−0.012 6	0.001 0
t=10	−0.004 3	0.006 6	0.015 2	−0.016 9**	−0.006 2	−0.005 1
t=11	−0.008 1	−0.015 2**	−0.009 7	−0.003 1	−0.004 6	0.017 8
t=12	0.006 3	0.009 2	0.009 9	0.002 4	−0.010 3	−0.014 8
Adjusted R^2	0.000 2	0.002 0	0.000 3	0.000 2	0.000 0	0.000 4
F-statistic	1.286 9	3.796 3	1.408 5	1.271 2	0.989 3	1.599 3
Prob(F-statistic)	0.149 3	0.000 0	0.080 9	0.160 7	0.478 5	0.027 2

***, ** and * stand for the significant level of 1%, 5%, and 10% respectively.

5.5.2 The Response of Unexpected Options Volumes of Different Options' Moneyness to News Announcements

The results obtained in the previous section are not only related with information effect of options trading volume, but also with transactions made for liquidity or hedging purposes. To investigate whether the predictive ability of options volume for the volatility of KOSPI200 index is attribute to the information trading, a direct test of the influence of news releases as direct measures of information on unexpected trading volume is performed. The Table 5-27 and Table 5-28 show the response of unexpected call options volume of different moneyness to good news and bad news respectively. As reported in the Table 5-27, the reactions of ATM and OTM call options to good news announcements are obviously stronger than other moneyness of options according to the value of F-statistic. Specially, the most coefficients for the response of OTM options to good news before news announcement are significantly positive. This result can be explained as the fact that OTM options is the best instrument for informed trading, with the intention of making a directional betting trade in a large stake. On the contrary, the significant reactions to the good news diminish after announcements. From another point of view, it also verifies the existence of information asymmetry. As shown in the Table 5-28, compared with the reaction of unexpected call option volumes to good news, the response of unexpected call option volumes to bad news is not obviously. However, it is obviously that the joint reaction of OTM options to the bad news is stronger in magnitude than the joint reaction of ATM options

Table 5-27　The Response of Unexpected Call Options Volume of Different Moneyness to Good News

	Good News Event				
	Deep ITM	ITM	ATM	OTM	Deep OTM
Constant	-217. 271 0	-683. 413 5	-23. 391 5	-126. 323 2	-32 796. 990 0
Return	64 889. 640 0	1 706 816. 000 0	-36 742. 660 0	-54 184. 130 0	14 032 253. 000 0
t=-12	-293. 673 4	-344. 084 0	-2 855. 241 0**	-3 861. 853 0**	-44 560. 390 0
t=-11	-299. 271 4	-944. 046 2	-6 248. 895 0***	-10 389. 510 0***	-55 427. 830 0
t=-10	-317. 690 6	-1 394. 300 0	-1 820. 467 0	-2 584. 005 0	10 797 197***
t=-9	-300. 106 2	-566. 790 1	14 654. 790 0***	33 663. 640 0***	-16 833. 400 0
t=-8	-329. 427 2	-247. 728 9	1 389. 759 0	5 712. 548 0***	-24 329. 500 0
t=-7	-313. 795 7	-181. 562 6	1 347. 014 0	10 354. 410 0***	-30 034. 310 0
t=-6	-323. 733 1	-664. 457 4	419. 098 1	3 813. 972**	-35 907. 040 0
t=-5	-319. 562 5	-965. 176 7	58. 815 9	1 325. 448***	-38 937. 850 0
t=-4	-288. 980 0	-696. 083 5	498. 110 3	4 415. 078 0	-36 609. 610 0
t=-3	-304. 374 3	-614. 691 4	1 546. 814 0	3 654. 809*	-37 248. 760 0
t=-2	-303. 319 1	-967. 346 5	-351. 160 5	534. 632 8	-42 288. 870 0
t=-1	-319. 351 2	-984. 754 1	-722. 717 0	429. 824 2	-44 724. 610 0
t=0	-718. 947 5	-13 292. 630 0	-578. 791 2	-3 167. 434 0	-145 100. 100 0

Table 5-27 (continued)

	Good News Event				
	Deep ITM	ITM	ATM	OTM	Deep OTM
t=1	-296. 493 9	-440. 600 3	-511. 785 2	2 052. 633 0	-42 878. 800 0
t=2	-309. 793 3	-165. 072 1	-607. 750 6	-1 933. 692 0	-39 843. 690 0
t=3	-299. 911 5	-588. 269 0	-136. 965 0	5. 870 7	-43 360. 770 0
t=4	-329. 152 9	-1 182. 641 0	186. 421 9	-1 743. 456 0	-45 713. 500 0
t=5	-330. 262 3	-975. 749 7	-1 973. 744 0	-4 000. 448*	-46 165. 020 0
t=6	-327. 764 5	-1 069. 671 0	-610. 917 9	853. 551 4	-46 310. 840 0
t=7	-319. 823 6	-553. 646 2	-1 471. 098 0	-459. 374 4	-46 224. 900 0
t=8	-323. 848 0	-530. 223 8	30. 655 7	-471. 637 8	-45 173. 800 0
t=9	-320. 460 9	-1 103. 934 0	-222. 517 6	-68. 926 1	-47 163. 120 0
t=10	-313. 448 3	-1 151. 554 0	-4 151. 472***	-6 242. 100***	-49 403. 280 0
t=11	-309. 171 0	-618. 770 8	-329. 573 4	-1 871. 843 0	-525 375. 600 0
t=12	-288. 541 8	-456. 374 3	8 752. 114***	5 116. 728***	-34 151. 830 0
Adjusted R^2	-0. 000 8	-0. 000 3	0. 004 4	0. 011 1	0. 004 1
F-statistic	0. 012 8	0. 559 6	7. 287 4	17. 021 2	6. 906 6
Prob(F-statistic)	1. 000 0	0. 965 0	0. 000 0	0. 000 0	0. 000 0

***, ** and * stand for the significant level of 1%, 5%, and 10% respectively.

Table 5-28 The Response of Unexpected Call Options Volume of Different Moneyness to Bad News

	Bad News Event				
	Deep ITM	ITM	ATM	OTM	Deep OTM
Constant	-235. 716 3	-1 335. 922 0	-25. 453 4	-26. 528 8	-6 521. 938 0
Return	60 600. 060 0	1 704 842***.	-41 782. 070 0	-68 496. 500 0	17 033 475. 000 0
t=-12	-269. 789 2	-564. 543 1	-2 760. 570 0**	-2 157. 855 0	-37 155. 740 0
t=-11	-451. 162 7	-58. 522 7	-6 976. 446 0***	-12 674. 450 0***	-108 067. 200 0
t=-10	-263. 046 9	181 868. 200***	-815. 146 5	1 328. 838 0	-103 964. 200 0
t=-9	-275. 786 6	-520. 455 1	4 646. 693 0***	14 490. 450 0***	-21 105. 450 0
t=-8	-493. 817 8	-1 231. 911 0	3 575. 210 0***	9 976. 739 0***	-48 376. 840 0
t=-7	-226. 291 8	-377. 115 9	1 423. 694 0	4 143. 180**	-25 975. 990 0
t=-6	-200. 271 5	-713. 867 1	1 180. 851 0	246. 340 0	-31 559. 280 0
t=-5	-201. 959 8	-678. 438 6	-833. 268 2	-839. 026 4	-30 829. 910 0
t=-4	-472. 140 4	-971. 897 4	565. 267 5	2 405. 555 0	-55 466. 550 0
t=-3	5 412. 470 0	-849. 522 7	-2 007. 506 0	-1 316. 914 0	-58 811. 680 0
t=-2	-482. 586 6	-767. 509 5	-191. 987 8	-1 656. 696 0	-62 931. 530 0
t=-1	-474. 565 7	-749. 241 4	-1 855. 017 0	-3 893. 244 0*	-66 538. 270 0
t=0	32. 628 8	13 682. 270 0	382. 000 8	1 650. 704 0	78 994. 890 0

Table 5-28 (continued)

	Bad News Event				
	Deep ITM	ITM	ATM	OTM	Deep OTM
t=1	-469. 369 0	-196. 271 8	-43. 866 8	-626. 522 0	-57 918. 080 0
t=2	-458. 352 5	-1 554. 532 0	4 150. 851 0	2 119. 537 0	-69 562. 330 0
t=3	-457. 745 6	-654. 648 8	683. 927 2	-1 730. 475 0	-64 013. 170 0
t=4	-461. 317 5	-1 073. 476 0	-101. 869 4	85. 132 2	-67 749. 520 0
t=5	-452. 843 2	-799. 779 2	-1 128. 038 0	-2 341. 262 0	-66 277. 880 0
t=6	-465. 175 8	-479. 274 4	1 824. 344 0	-1 142. 959 0	-64 892. 920 0
t=7	-427. 860 2	160. 205 2	606. 775 3	1 534. 900 0	-63 038. 280 0
t=8	-454. 346 6	-1 040. 665 0	-64. 625 8	-1 365. 728 0	-74 040. 430 0
t=9	-497. 516 5	-1 208. 876 0	-1 703. 475 0	-2 338. 373 0	-77 067. 370 0
t=10	-454. 015 7	-242. 452 5	-3 561. 686 0**	-8 996. 932 0***	-64 349. 150 0
t=11	-450. 018 3	-7 448. 150 0	906. 755 1	-3 880. 129*	4 039 406. 000 0***
t=12	-455. 846 4	-2 294. 055 0	10 717. 830 0***	15 709. 530 0***	-49 554. 600 0
Adjusted R^2	-0. 000 7	0. 004 1	0. 002 4	0. 006 3	-0. 000 2
F-statistic	0. 058 3	6. 844 7	4. 465 0	9. 946 8	0. 773 7
Prob(F-statistic)	1. 000 0	0. 000 0	0. 000 0	0. 000 0	0. 786 0

***, ** and * stand for the significant level of 1%, 5%, and 10% respectively.

to the bad news announcement. It maybe account for the fact that informed trader will prefer to choose OTM call options to set their investment strategy when they have acquired private information on bad news.

According to Blasco et al. (2010), in presence of informed trading, there is higher incentive for traders to buy put options to realize their strategy. So it is necessary to investigate the reaction of the unexpected volume of put options to the news announcement. The Table 5 - 29 and Table 5 - 30 show the responses of unexpected put options volume of different moneyness to good news and bad news. The results differ somewhat between call and put options. As reported in the Table 5-29, the partial coefficients for the response of only ATM options to good news before news announcement are significant and the news impact reflected in the ATM put options trading volume is stronger than that reflected in the ATM call options. It is obviously that ATM put options are attractive to the informed trader, regardless of good news and bad news announcement. That is because that no matter the news is good or bad, once news is announced, it is bound to give rise to the increase in the volatility of the KOSPI200 index. Because ATM options are sensitivity to the volatility, if informed traders use the ATM option to carry out their investment plan, they will acquire high profit. Conversely it is hard to find there is significant relation between unexpected put volumes of other options moneyness and the news announcement. It therefore appears that trading volume in other moneyness of options may be linked to factors other than news, such as high liquidity, while ATM options are related with the informed trading. These results are consistent with the finding of Ni, Pan & Poteshman (2008), who argue that investors with volatility information prefer at-the-money to the other moneyness of options because of lower bid-ask spread and higher sensitivity to volatility. These results also provide indirect evidence on the existence of informed volatility trading. Unlike traders with directional information about underlying asset, investors with information about future volatility will choose at-the-money options instead of out-the-money options to set their investment strategy. On the other hand, the estimator for out-the-money options only at t=-10 is significant. In general, the result of Table 5-29 not only provides empirical evidence on the existence of information asymmetry in the Korean Security Markets, but also further confirms that the predictive power of the options volume for the future volatility should attribute to the informed trading rather than other purposes. Contrary to the exception, the reaction of unexpected options volume to bad news is not stronger than to good news. The result of Table 5-30 is consistent with the finding of Hong & Stein (1999), suggesting that investors may promptly trade before or after good news, but the reaction is slower when the bad news is announced. It can be rationally explained by the fact that the investors need some time to deliberate their investment strategy and decide whether to sell the shareholding that they have before bad news are announced. As shown in the Table 5-30, the reaction of OTM put options to bad news is much stronger than other options' moneyness. These results are somewhat different from the finding of call options volumes, but the findings are not surprising. These findings for the relationship between unexpected put options volume and bad news are consistent with the argument of Branger & Schlag (2005). Investors showing a high level of loss aversion and a strong incentive to hedge against natural disasters or sudden market shocks are the main traders in this type of product based on OTM put options. An informed investor of these characteristics displays high sensitivity to bad news, which explains the statistical significance of bad news in OTM options. This argument is also directly linked to the presence of short sales constraints.

In this section a direct test of the influence of news releases as direct measures of information on unexpected put-call ratio of different moneyness is performed. As reported in the Table 5-31, the reactions of unexpected put-call ratio of ATM and OTM options to good news announcements are obviously stronger than other options moneyness according to the value of F-statistic. Specially, the most coefficients for the response of ATM options to good news before announcement are significant. However, the significant reactions to the good news diminish after announcements. From another point of view, it also verifies the existence of information asymmetry. Compared with the reaction of unexpected put-call ratio to good news, the response of unexpected put-call ratio to bad news is not notable. The Table 5 - 32 shows the response of unexpected put-call ratio of different options moneyness to bad news. The results indicate that informed trader prefer ATM and deep OTM to achieve their investment strategy when they master the upcoming bad news.

In general, the reaction of ATM to news announcement is strongest and quickest, followed by deep OTM and OTM options. This result maybe attribute to the cause that volatility informed traders are in fond of using ATM options as useful avenue for their investment, while OTM and deep OTM options are preferred by directional informed trader.

Table 5-29 The Response of Unexpected of Put Options Volume of Different Moneyness to Good News

	Good News Event				
	Deep ITM	ITM	ATM	OTM	Deep OTM
Constant	2.017 9	-4.351 5	-7.302 2	-20 950.100 0	-10 195.570 0
Return	24 573.640 0	2 605.063 0	30 031.060 0	52 206 676.000 0***	-73 047 993.000 0
t=-12	-165.712 9	307.291 0	-4 106.656 0**	-34 284.990 0	-259 497.300 0
t=-11	-174.061 1	244.665 4	-6 811.059 0***	-61 291.320 0	-237 852.900 0
t=-10	-202.816 7	214.176 3	-2 497.836*	-67 603.570 0	10 297 576.000 0
t=-9	-185.486 7	214.595 4	7 927.646 0***	-26 794.000 0	-218 547.000 0
t=-8	-186.469 6	147.011 7	3 948.378 0**	-21 502.360 0	-251 356.300 0
t=-7	-166.710 0	136.279 9	1 724.731 0	-18 509.640 0	-265 096.200 0
t=-6	-165.743 4	125.559 0	771.752 9	-32 639.740 0	-248 574.000 0
t=-5	-169.082 2	187.776 7	1 380.419 0	-35 716.360 0	-245 671.300 0
t=-4	-171.866 9	-39.182 7	1 417.359 0	-28 532.190 0	-259 676.500 0
t=-3	-198.264 8	-94.761 8	347.292 1	-27 615.160 0	-260 344.300 0
t=-2	-207.540 1	-48.492 8	150.990 1	-35 053.170 0	-252 681.400 0
t=-1	-190.418 5	-80.218 3	-624.356 2	-33 738.740 0	-254 403.900 0
t=0	-289.653 1	-163.195 2	-1 305.740 0	-412 442.000 0	268 224.000 0

Table 5-29 (continued)

	Good News Event				
	Deep ITM	ITM	ATM	OTM	Deep OTM
t=1	-142. 772 9	34. 914 9	-409. 751 4	-20 873. 260 0	-278 428. 100 0
t=2	-143. 941 4	-85. 333 3	-751. 637 4	-15 774. 750 0	-290 251. 100 0
t=3	-159. 798 1	-33. 693 8	195. 440 0	-26 891. 590 0	-278 849. 500 0
t=4	-201. 391 2	-58. 435 9	379. 247 2	-45 217. 680 0	-251 318. 600 0
t=5	-183. 029 1	-129. 001 2	-1 016. 449 0	-37 610. 990 0	-265 935. 100 0
t=6	3 743. 994 0	-101. 205 3	-1 148. 770 0	-40 635. 920 0	-262 155. 700 0
t=7	-184. 572 8	-25. 121 2	-525. 715 8	-25 445. 080 0	-280 433. 900 0
t=8	-158. 240 2	514. 935 7	-563. 072 8	-26 396. 760 0	-278 216. 400 0
t=9	-155. 011 8	-70. 017 4	1 497. 274 0	-41 563. 530 0	-244 366. 100 0
t=10	-170. 265 4	-21. 872 9	-2 388. 163 0	-47 613. 240 0	-228 583. 200 0
t=11	-175. 285 2	-40. 643 0	848. 644 0	-31 866. 470 0	-728 338. 800 0
t=12	-159. 587 8	49. 674 2	3 502. 897 0***	-18 005. 710 0	-243 691. 800 0
Adjusted R^2	-0. 000 4	-0. 000 3	0. 001 6	-0. 000 3	0. 000 1
F-statistic	0. 489 7	0. 620 6	3. 279 3	0. 556 6	1. 169 6
Prob(F-statistic)	0. 986 2	0. 932 8	0. 000 0	0. 966 2	0. 251 1

*** , ** and * stand for the significant level of 1% , 5%, and 10% respectively.

Table 5-31 The Response of Unexpected Put-Call Ratio of Different Moneyness to Good News

	Good News Event				
	Deep ITM	ITM	ATM	OTM	Deep OTM
Constant	0.000 8	0.000 4	0.000 1	0.000 5	−0.000 4
Return	0.754 5	0.183 7	0.517 8***	0.417 0*	0.031 3
t=−12	−0.021 4	−0.033 261**	−0.008 8	−0.003 6	0.002 8
t=−11	0.003 1	−0.006 7	−0.025 4***	−0.024 3**	−0.036 9***
t=−10	0.016 8	0.004 9	−0.057 6***	−0.056 3***	−0.003 1
t=−9	0.005 0	−0.010 1	−0.005 4	−0.023 4**	−0.009 2
t=−8	−0.021 2	0.006 0	0.023 0***	0.008 4	−0.002 2
t=−7	−0.013 7	−0.021 3	0.024 8***	−0.002 3	0.008 4
t=−6	−0.038 4	−0.001 0	0.005 8	0.003 9	0.013 9
t=−5	−0.044 1*	0.027 2	0.016 2*	0.008 4	−0.002 0
t=−4	−0.006 3	0.003 5	0.003 1	0.003 5	0.008 3
t=−3	−0.009 3	−0.005 4	−0.006 7	−0.004 5	−0.010 3
t=−2	−0.034 9	0.018 6	0.012 0	−0.009 9	0.009 0
t=−1	0.017 5	0.011 9	−0.009 6	−0.005 9	0.023 5**
t=0	−0.014 4	−0.022 6	−0.004 2	−0.003 7	0.006 8

Table 5-31 (continued)

	Good News Event				
	Deep ITM	ITM	ATM	OTM	Deep OTM
t=1	-0. 028 1	0. 017 4	-0. 007 1	-0. 006 9	-0. 013 8
t=2	0. 047 4	-0. 032 5	0. 011 5	-0. 018 2	0. 003 5
t=3	-0. 004 5	0. 016 8	0. 002 1	-0. 015 9	0. 005 2
t=4	0. 004 7	0. 015 2	0. 009 0	0. 000 1	-0. 005 0
t=5	-0. 037 5	-0. 004 5	-0. 012 8	0. 001 8	0. 020 5
t=6	0. 033 9	-0. 024 1	-0. 001 5	-0. 010 3	0. 000 5
t=7	-0. 039 6	-0. 014 2	0. 005 6	0. 010 2	0. 025 4**
t=8	-0. 036 0	-0. 014 9	-0. 018 5*	-0. 001 1	0. 020 4
t=9	0. 035 7	0. 022 3	0. 011 1	-0. 010 9	0. 014 9
t=10	-0. 028 8	-0. 023 3	-0. 016 6**	-0. 006 2	0. 016 5
t=11	-0. 003 9	-0. 038 5**	0. 005 9	0. 010 2	-0. 003 6
t=12	0. 012 7	0. 009 2	0. 006 4	0. 015 4**	0. 005 8
Adjusted R^2	0. 000 0	0. 000 1	0. 002 2	0. 001 4	0. 000 0
F-statistic	1. 034 2	1. 179 8	4. 065 3	2. 956 4	1. 055 3
Prob(F-statistic)	0. 415 2	0. 240 7	0. 000 0	0. 000 0	0. 386 7

***, ** and * stand for the significant level of 1%, 5%, and 10% respectively.

Table 5-32 The Response of Unexpected Put-Call Ratio of Different Moneyness to Bad News

	Bad News Event				
	Deep ITM	ITM	ATM	OTM	Deep OTM
Constant	-0.000 1	-0.000 2	-0.000 1	-0.000 2	0.000 5
Return	0.583 3	0.095 3	0.453 9	0.407 0**	0.060 9
t=-12	-0.002 6	0.014 2	0.010 8**	-0.000 9	0.005 1
t=-11	-0.001 5	0.011 1	-0.003 5	-0.012 7	-0.054 2***
t=-10	0.005 0	-0.002 7	0.040 3***	0.008 3	-0.029 2**
t=-9	-0.006 3	0.000 7	0.004 4	0.006 6	-0.007 4
t=-8	-0.013 9	0.013 3	0.015 4	0.018 6*	-0.041 7***
t=-7	-0.026 8	0.003 9	0.000 6	0.006 5	-0.011 4
t=-6	0.005 1	0.001 5	0.001 8	0.016 5	0.008 4
t=-5	-0.002 3	-0.002 5	-0.007 7	-0.003 5	-0.016 4
t=-4	-0.018 0	0.008 6	0.005 5	0.000 9	-0.013 4
t=-3	-0.043 8	-0.010 3	0.000 6	0.002 6	0.010 7
t=-2	0.047 5	-0.008 2	-0.011 2	0.005 1	0.015 0
t=-1	0.004 3	0.037 9**	0.007 7	0.009 8	-0.016 3
t=0	-0.018 1	0.001 4	-0.005 5	0.008 7	-0.000 3

Table 5-32 (continued)

	Bad News Event				
	Deep ITM	ITM	ATM	OTM	Deep OTM
t=1	0.023 4	0.004 0	0.001 9	−0.001 0	0.000 6
t=2	−0.026 7	0.017 8	−0.011 4	0.001 0	−0.021 5
t=3	−0.014 1	−0.004 1	−0.002 2	0.000 2	0.006 4
t=4	0.015 1	0.016 3	−0.004 6	−0.000 5	0.002 5
t=5	0.001 1	0.013 1	−0.017 1	−0.006 5	0.011 7
t=6	−0.005 4	−0.000 8	0.009 0	0.002 7	−0.004 3
t=7	0.046 8	−0.015 7	−0.002 5	0.003 5	0.017 7
t=8	0.000 5	−0.040 0	0.004 1	0.005 9	0.010 7
t=9	0.039 4	0.017 6	−0.002 8	−0.003 0	−0.032 7
t=10	0.010 6	−0.002 0	−0.015 0	−0.004 3	−0.007 8
t=11	0.025 4	−0.006 0	−0.011 1	0.014 8	0.001 4
t=12	−0.007 4	−0.004 5	0.019 6***	−0.009 3	−0.005 8
Adjusted R^2	−0.000 3	−0.000 3	0.001 1	−0.000 1	0.000 6
F-statistic	0.641 2	0.569 1	2.618 7	0.900 5	1.829 9
Prob(F-statistic)	0.918 6	0.960 9	0.000 0	0.609 4	0.006 1

***, ** and * stand for the significant level of 1%, 5%, and 10% respectively.

6 Conclusion

This study attempts to explore the predictive power of options volume for the volatility of KOSPI200 index, by testing the dynamic relations between the volatility of the KOSPI200 index and options trading volume. The volatility of the index is approximated by EGARCH method. Using a VAR equation model to capture the volume – volatility relations, this study finds strong and unambiguous evidence on the predictive power of option volumes for the volatility of KOSPI200. Similarly, lagged changes in volatility have a significant predictive power for option volume, although the influence is not strong as expected. In order to capture the activity of informed trader, the signals obtained from option volume are partitioned into expected components and unexpected components to further investigate the process of informed trading. This research shows that the predictive ability of unexpected options volume with respect to the volatility of KOSPI200 index is much stronger than the overall options volume. This finding provides distinct empirical evidence on the existence of informed trading.

Considering the different influence of various investors on the movement of spot equity market, it is necessary to investigate the information role of various investors for the volatility of KOSPI200 index. In this research, the investors are divided into three classifications: foreign investors, individual investors and institutional investors. The findings of this study also suggest that foreign institutional investors have strongest predictive power in the Korean option market, thereby providing evidence that foreign investors do indeed have superior ability to collect and analyze information than individual investors and institutional investors.

Motivated by the fact that different degrees of options moneyness have various influences on informed investors when making the choice, it appears reasonable to investigate the informational content of different degree of options moneyness. For call options, this study finds that OTM and ATM call options provide the best measure of the volatility of KOSPI200 index. Likewise, for put options, this study also validates that ATM and deep OTM put options have best predictive power for the volatility of KOSPI200 index.

Finally, most of the previous studies on the information content of options volume regard the assumption that the options volume serves as good proxy for informed trading as premise of their studies. There is scant evidence, however, of any attempt to test this assumption directly. The most novel feature of this study is that this research attempts to focus on whether the predictive power of options volume and put-call ratio for the volatility of KOSPI200 index can be attributed to informed trading rather than other reason, such as liquidity or hedge. In other words, this study seeks to determine whether the change of options volume occurs as a result of the release of news, a claim that has been taken as a premise in the literature but has never been directly proved. The results of this research show that the predictive power of options volume for the volatility is indeed attributed to the informed trading. This research also finds that the reaction of the unexpected options volumes of foreign institutional investors to news announcement is strongest, thereby providing rational explanation on the predictive power of foreign investor for the volatility of KOSPI200. In addition, this research confirms that the reaction of ATM to news announcement is strongest and quickest, followed by deep OTM and OTM options. This finding also supports the hypothesis that ATM and OTM are preferred by the informed trader.

The main results of this study suggest that the trading volume of KOSPI200 index options has strong predictive ability with respect to the future volatility of the KOSPI200 index, and that the markets for KOSPI200 index options are venues for informed trading. This research not only provides an important implication for academics and practical guidelines for studies on the relation between options volume and the volatility of spot index, but also may provoke further study of the information content of index options market, although it is generally viewed as being less informative than individual stock markets. However, evidence on the investment strategy of volatility informed trading, such as straddle strategy, is not given in this study. This remains to be seen in the future research.

References

ADMATI A, PFLEIDERER P, 1988. A theory of intraday patterns: Volume and price variability[J]. Review of financial studies, 1: 3-40.

AHN H J, BAE K H, CHAN K, 2001. Limit orders, depth, and volatility [J]. Journal of finance, 56: 767-788.

AHN H, KANG J, RYU D, 2008. Informed trading in the index option market: The case of KOSPI 200 options[J]. Journal of futures markets, 28: 1118-1146.

ÄIJO J, 2008. Impact of US and UK macroeconomic news announcements on the return distribution implied by FTSE - 100 index options [J]. International review of financial analysis, 17: 242-258.

ALBUQUERQUE R, VEGA C, 2009. Economic news and international stock market comovement[J]. Review of finance, 13: 401-465.

ALI A, HWANG L S, TROMBLEY M A, 2003. Arbitrage risk and the book

-to-market anomaly[J]. Journal of financial economics, 69: 355-73.

ALIZADEH S, BRANDT M W, DIEBOLD F X, 2002. Range - based estimation of stochastic volatility models[J]. Journal of finance, 57: 1047-1091.

AMIN K I, LEE C M C, 1997. Option trading, price discovery, and earnings news dissemination[J]. Contemporary accounting research, 14: 153-192.

ANAND A, CHAKRAVARTY S, 2007. Stealth trading in options markets [J]. Journal of financial and quantitative analysis, 42: 167-188.

ANAND A., CHAKRAVARTY S, MARTELL T, 2005. Empirical evidence on the evolution of liquidity: choice of market versus limit orders by informed and uninformed traders[J]. Journal of financial markets, 8: 289-309.

ANDERSEN T G, 1996. Return volatility and trading volume: An information flow interpretation of stochastic volatility[J]. Journal of finance, 51: 169-204.

ANDERSEN T G, BOLLERSLEV T, 1998. Answering the skeptics: Yes, standard volatility models do provide accurate forecasts[J]. International economic review, 39: 885-905.

ANDERSEN T G, BOLLERSLEV T, 1999, Forecasting financial market volatility: Sample frequency vis-a-vis forecast horizon [J]. Journal of empirical finance, 6 (5): 457-477.

ANDERSEN T G, BOLLERSLEV T, 1998. Deutschmark-dollar volatility: intra-day activity patterns, macroeconomic announcements, and longer-run dependencies[J]. Journal of finance, 53: 219-265.

ANDERSEN T G, BOLLERSLEV T, 2001. The distribution of realized exchange rate volatility[J]. Journal of the american statistical association, 96: 42-55.

ANDERSON H M, VAHID F, 2007. Forecasting the volatility of Australian stock returns: Do common factors help[J]. Journal of business & economic statistics, 25(1): 34-45.

ANGELIDIS T, A BENOS, 2009. The components of the bid-ask spread: The case of the Athens stock exchange [J]. European financial management, 15: 112-144.

ANTHONY J H, 1988. The interrelation of stock and options market trading-volume data[J]. Journal of finance, 43(4): 949-964.

ANTONIOU A, HOLMES P, 1995. Futures trading, information and spot price volatility: Evidence for the FTSE-100 stock index futures contract using GARCH[J]. Journal of banking and finance, 19: 117-129.

ARROW K J, 1964. The role of securities in the optimal allocation of risk-bearing[J]. Review of economics studies, 31: 91-96.

BACK K, 1993. Asymmetric information and options[J]. review of financial studies, 6: 435-472.

BADRINATH S, WAHAL S, 2002. Momentum trading by institutions[J]. Journal of finance, 57: 2449-2478.

BAE K H, JANG H, PARK K S, 2003. Traders' choice between limit and market orders: evidence from NYSE stocks[J]. Journal of financial markets, 6: 517-538.

BAGEHOT W, 1971. The only game in town[J]. Financial analysts journal, 27: 31-35.

BAGNOLI M, KROSS W, WATTS S, 2002. The information in management's expected earnings report data: A day late, a penny short[J]. Journal of accounting research, 40: 1275-1296.

BAI C, LIU Q, LU J, SONG F M, ZHANG J, 2005. Corporate governance and market valuation in China[J]. Journal of comparative economics, 32: 599-616.

BAKSHI G, CAO C, CHEN Z W, 1997. Empirical performance of alternative option pricing models[J]. Journal of finance, 52: 2003-2049.

BAKSHI G, CAO C, CHEN Z W, 2000. Do call prices and the underlying stock, always move in the same direction[J]. Review of financial studies, 13: 549-584.

BAKSHI G S, CAO C, CHEN Z W, 2000. Pricing and hedging long-term options[J]. Journal of econometrics, 94: 277-318.

BAKSHI G, KAPADIA N, 2003. Delta-hedged gains and the negative market volatility risk premium[J]. Review of financial studies, 16: 527-566.

BALDUZZI P, ELTON E, GREEN T, 2001. Economic news and bond prices. Journal of financial and quantitative analysis, 36: 523-543.

BALL C, ROMA A, 1994. Stochastic volatility option pricing[J]. Journal of financial and quantitative analysis, 29: 589-607.

BANERJEE P S, DORAN J S, PETERSON D R, 2007. Implied volatility and future portfolio returns[J]. Journal of banking and finance, 31: 3183-3199.

BARBER B M, LEE Y T, LIU Y J, ODEAN T, 2007. Is the aggregate investor reluctant to realize losses? evidence from Taiwan[J]. European financial management, 13: 423-447.

BARBER B M, ODEAN T, 2000. Trading is hazardous to your wealth: The common stock investment performance of individual investors[J]. Journal of finance, 55 (2): 773-806.

BARBER B M, ODEAN T, ZHU N, 2009. Do retail trades move markets [J]. Review of financial studies, 22: 151-186.

BARBER B, LEE Y T, LIU Y J, ODEAN T, 2009. Just how much do individual investor loss by trading [J]. Review of financial studies, 22: 609-632.

BARBERIS N, SHLEIFER A, VISHNY R, 1998, A model of investor sentiment [J]. Journal of financial economics, 49: 307-343

BARCLAY M J, WARNER J B, 1993. Stealth trading and volatility: which trades move prices [J]. Journal of financial economics, 34: 281-305.

BATES D, 1991. The crash of '87: Was it expected? The evidence from options market [J]. Journal of finance, 46: 1009-1044.

BATES D S, 1996. Jumps and stochastic volatility: exchange rate processes implicit in PHLX Deutsche mark options [J]. Review of financial studies, 9: 69-107.

BAUER G, VEGA C, 2008. The monetary origins of asymmetric information in international equity markets [J]. Journal of international money and finance, 27: 1029-1055.

BECKER K, FINNERTY J, FRIEDMAM J, 1995. Economic news and equity market linkages between the U.S. and U.K[J]. Journal of banking and finance, 19: 1191-1210.

BECKER R, CLEMENTS A E, 2008. Are combination forecasts of S&P 500 volatility statistically superior[J]. International journal of forecasting, 24: 122-133.

BECKER R, CLEMENTS A E, WHITE S I, 2007. Does implied volatility provide any information beyond that captured in model-based volatility forecasts? [J]. Journal of banking and finance, 31: 2535-2549.

BECKERS S, 1981. Standard deviations implied in option prices as predictors of future stock price variability[J]. Journal of banking and finance, 5: 363-382.

BEKAERT G H, HARVEY C R, 1997. Emerging equity market volatility[J]. Journal of financial economics, 43: 29-77.

BENVENISTE L M, MARCUS A J, WILHELM W I, 1992. What's special about the Specialist[J]. Journal of financial economics, 32: 61-86.

BERNDT E, HALL B, HALL R, HAUSMAN J, 1974. Estimation and inference in nonlinear structural models[J]. Annals of social measurement, 3: 653-665.

BESSEMBINDER H, SEGUIN P J, 1992. Futures trading activity and stock price volatility[J]. Journal of finance, 47: 2015–2034.

BHATTACHARYA M, 1987. Price changes of related securities: The case of call options and stock[J]. Journal of financial and quantitative analysis, 22: 1–15.

BHUYAN R, YAN Y, 2002. Informational role of open interests and volumes: Evidence from option markets[J]. Paper presented at Twelfth Annual Asia–Pacific futures research symposium held in Bangkok, 23–31.

BIAIS B, HILLION P, 1994. Insider and liquidity trading in stock and options markets[J]. Review of financial studies, 74: 743–780.

BIAIS B, HILLION P, SPATT C, 1995. An empirical analysis of the limit order book and the order flow in the Paris Bourse[J]. Journal of finance, 50: 1655–1689.

BILLINGS M, JENNINGS R, 2011. The option market's anticipation of information content in earnings announcements[J]. Review of accounting studies, 16: 587–619.

BLACK F, 1975. Fact and fantasy in the use of options[J]. Financial analysts journal, 31(4): 36–72.

BLACK F, 1976. The pricing of commodity contracts[J]. Journal of financial economics, 3: 167–179.

BLACK F, SCHOLES M S, 1973. The pricing of options and corporate liabilities[J]. Journal of political economy, 81: 637-659.

BLAIR B J, POON S, TAYLOR S J, 2001. Forecasting S&P 100 volatility: The incremental information content of implied volatilities and high—frequency index returns[J]. Journal of econometrics, 105: 5-26.

BLASCO N, CORREDOR P, DEL Rı'O C, SANTAMARı'A R, 2005. Bad news and Dow Jones make the Spanish stocks go round[J]. European journal of operational research, 163: 253-275.

BLASCO N, CORREDOR P, SANTAMARı'A R, 2010. Does informed trading occur in the options market? Some revealing clues[J]. Accounting and finance, 50: 555-579

BLISS R, PANIGIRTZOGLOU N, 2002. Testing the stability of implied probability density functions[J]. Journal of banking and finance, 26: 381-422.

BLOOMFIELD R, ÖHARA M, SAAR G, 2005. The make or take decision in an electronic market: evidence on the evolution of liquidity[J]. Journal of financial economics, 75: 165-199.

BOHL M, BRZESZCZYNSKI J, 2006. Do institutional investors destabilize stock prices? Evidence from an emerging market [J]. Journal of international financial markets, institutions and money, 16: 370-383.

BOLLEN N P B, WHALEY R E, 2004. Does net buying pressure affect the shape of implied volatility functions[J]. The journal of finance, 59: 711-753.

BOLLERSLEV T, 1986. Generalized autoregressive conditional heteroskedasticity[J]. Journal of econometrics, 31: 307-327.

BOLLERSLEV T, 1990. Modeling the coherence in short-run nominal exchange rates: a multivariate generalized ARCH model[J]. Review of economics and statistics, 72:498-505.

BOLLERSLEV T, WOOLDRIDGE J M, 1992. Quasi-maximum likelihood estimation and inference in dynamic models with time-varying covariances [J]. Econometric reviews, 11: 143-172.

BOYER B, ZHENG L, 2009. Investor flows and stock market returns[J]. Journal of empirical finance, 16: 87-100.

BOYLE P P, 1988. A lattice framework for option pricing with two state variables[J]. Journal of financial and quantitative analysis, 23: 1-12.

BOYLE P, EMANUEL D, 1980. Discretely adjusted option hedges[J]. Journal of financial economics, 8: 259-282.

BRAILSFORD T J, FAFF R W, 1996. An evaluation of volatility forecasting techniques[J]. Journal of banking and finance, 20: 419-438.

BREEDEN D, LITZENBERGER R, 1978. Prices of state contingent claims implicit in option prices[J]. Journal of business, 51: 621-651.

BRENNAN M, CAO H, 1996. Information, trade, and derivative securities [J]. Review of financial studies, 9: 163-208.

BRENNAN M J, CAO H, 1997. International portfolio flows[J]. Journal of finance, 52: 1851-1880.

BRENNER M, GALAI D, 1989. New financial instruments for hedging changes in volatility[J]. Financial analysts journal, 4: 61-65.

BRENNER M, GALAI D, 1993. Hedging volatility in foreign currencies[J]. Journal of derivatives, 1: 53-59.

BRITTEN M, NEUBERGER A, 2000. Option prices, implied price processes, and stochastic volatility[J]. Journal of finance, 55: 839-866.

BROCK W A, LEBARON B D, 1996. A dynamic structural model for stock return volatility and trading volume[J]. Review of economics and statistics, 78(1): 94-110.

BROOKS C, 1998. Predicting stock index volatility: Can market volume help [J]. Journal of forecasting, 17(1): 59-80.

Brooks C, 2008. Introductory Econometrics for Finance[M]. UK: Cambridge

University Press.

BROWN C, ROBINSON D, 2002. Skewness and kurtosis implied by option prices: A correction[J]. Journal of financial research, 25: 279-282.

BROWN G W, CLIFF M T, 2004. Investor sentiment and the near-term stock market[J]. Journal of empirical finance, 11: 1-27.

BROWN P, WALSH D M, YUEN A, 1997. The interaction of order imbalance and stock price[J]. Pacific basin finance journal, 5: 539-557.

BROWN R L, SHEVLIN T J, 1983. Option and stock market efficiency[J]. Australian journal of management, 8: 71-87.

CAI F, ZHENG L, 2004. Institutional trading and stock returns[J]. Finance research letters, 1: 178-189.

CAMPBELL J, RAMODORAI T, SCHWARTZ A, 2009. Caught on tape: institutional trading, stock returns, and earnings announcements [J]. Journal of financial economics, 92: 66-91.

CANINA L, FIGLEWSKI S, 1993. The informational content of implied volatility[J]. Review of financial studies, 6: 659-681.

CAO C, CHEN Z, GRIFFIN J, 2005. Informational content of option volume prior to takeovers[J]. Journal of business, 78: 1073-1109.

CAO C, HANSCH O, WANG X, 2008. Order placement strategies in a pure limit order book market[J]. Journal of financial research, 31: 113-140.

CAO M, WEI J, 2010. Option market liquidity: Commonality and other characteristics[J]. Journal of financial markets, 13: 20-48,

CERRATO M, SARANTIS N, SAUNDERS A, 2011. An investigation of costumer order flow in the foreign exchange market[J]. Journal of banking and finance, 35: 1892-1906.

CHAKRAVARTY S, 2001. Stealth-trading: Which traders' trades move stock prices[J]. Journal of financial economics, 61: 289-307.

CHAKRAVARTY S, GULEN H, MAYHEW S, 2005. ''Informed trading in stock and option markets[J]. Journal of finance, 59: 1235-1258.

CHAKRAVARTY S, HOLDEN C, 1995. An integrated model of market and limit orders[J]. Journal of financial intermediation, 4: 213-241.

CHAN K, 1992. A furher analysis of the lead-lag relationship between the cash market and stock index futures market [J]. Review of financial studies, 5: 123-152.

CHAN K, CHUNG P Y, 1993. Intraday relationships among index arbitrage, spot and futures price volatility, and spot market volume: A transaction data set[J]. Journal of banking and finance, 17: 663-687.

CHAN K, CHUNG Y P, FONG W M, 2002. The informational role of stock and option volume[J]. Review of financial studies, 15: 1049-1075.

CHAN K, CHUNG P Y, JOHNSON H, 1993. Why option prices lag stock prices: A trading-based explanation[J]. Journal of finance, 48: 1957-1968.

CHAN K C, CHANG Y, LUNG P P, 2009. Informed trading under different market conditions and moneyness: Evidence from TXO options[J]. Pacific-basin finance journal, 17(2) :189-208.

CHAN L K C, LAKONISHOK J, 1993. Institutional trades and intraday stock price behavior[J]. Journal of financial economics, 33: 173-199.

CHAN L K C, LAKONISHOK J, 1995. The behavior of stock prices around institutional trades[J]. Journal of finance, 50: 1147-1174.

CHANG C, 2010. Herding and the role of foreign institutions in emerging equity markets[J]. Pacific-Basin finance journal, 18: 175-185.

CHANG C C, HSEI P F, LAI H N, 2009. Do informed option investors predict stock returns? Evidence from the Taiwan stock exchange [J]. Journal of banking & finance, 33(4): 757-764.

CHARI A, OUIMET P P, TESAR L L, 2010. The returns to developed-market acquirers in emerging markets[J]. Review of financial studies, 23: 1741-1770.

CHATRATH A, RAMCHANDER S, SONG F, 1995. Does options trading lead to greater cash market volatility[J]. The journal of futures markets, 15: 785-803.

CHATRATH A, RAMCHANDER S, SONG F, 1996. The role of futures trading activity in exchange rate[J]. The journal of futures markets, 16: 561-584.

CHEN C R, LUNG P P, TAY N S P, 2005. Information flow between the stock and option markets: Where do informed traders trade[J]. Review of financial economics, 14: 1-23.

CHEN L, JOHNSON S, LIN J, LIU Y, 2009. Information, sophistication, and foreign versus domestic investors' performance[J]. Journal of banking and finance, 33: 1636-1651.

CHIRAC D P, MANASTER S, 1978. The information content of market prices and a test of market efficiency[J]. Journal of financial economics, 6: 213-234.

CHIYACHANTANA C N, JAIN P K, JIANG C, WOOD R A, 2004. International evidence on institutional trading behavior and price impact [J]. The journal of finance, 59: 869-898.

CHOE H, CHUNG J, LEE W, 2008. Distribution of private information across investors: Evidence from the Korea Stock Exchange [J]. Asia-pacific journal of financial studies, 37: 101-137.

CHOE H, EOM Y, 2009. The disposition effect and investment performance in the futures market[J]. Journal of futures markets, 29 (6): 496-522.

CHOE H, KHO B C, STULZ R M, 1999. Do foreign investors destabilize stock markets? The Korean experience in 1997 [J]. Journal of financial economics, 54: 227-264.

CHOE H, KHO B C, STULZ R M, 2005. Do domestic investors have an edge? The trading experience of foreign investors in Korea[J]. Review of financial studies, 18: 795-829.

CHONG Y Y, HENDRY D F, 1986. Econometric evaluation of linear macroeconomic models[J]. Review of economic studies, 53: 671-690.

CHORDIA T, 2009. Theory-based illiquidity and asset pricing[J]. Review of financial studies, 22(9): 3629-3668.

CHRISTENSEN B J, HANSEN C S, 2002. New evidence on the implied-realized volatility relation[J]. The European journal of finance, 8: 187-205.

CHRISTENSEN B J, PRABHALA N, 1998. The relation between implied and realized volatility[J]. Journal of financial economics, 50: 125-150.

CHRISTIE A, 1982. The stochastic behaviour of common stock variances; value, leverage and interest rate effects[J]. Journal of financial economics, 10: 213-234.

CHUANG W, SUSMEL R, 2011. Who is the more overconfident trader? Individual vs. institutional investors[J]. Journal of banking and finance, 35: 1626-1644.

CHUNG K H, VANNESS B F, VANNESS R A, 1999. Limit orders and the bid-ask spread[J]. Journal of financial economics, 53: 255-287.

CLARK P K, 1973. A subordinated stochastic process model with finite variance for speculative prices[J]. Econometrica, 41: 135-155.

CLEMEN R T, 1989. Combining forecasts: A review and annotated bibliography[J]. International journal of forecasting, 5(4): 559-583.

COHEN R, GOMPERS P, VUOLTEENAHO T, 2002. Who underreacts to cash-flow news? Evidence from trading between individuals and institutions [J]. Journal of financial economics, 66: 40-462.

COPELAND T E, 1976. A model of asset trading under the assumption of sequential information arrival[J]. Journal of finance, 31(4): 1149-1168.

COPELAND T, GALAI D, 1983. Information effects on the bid-ask spread [J]. Journal of finance, 38: 1457-1469.

CORRADO C J, MILLER T W, 2005. The forecast quality of CBOE implied volatility indexes[J]. Journal of futures markets, 25(4): 339-373.

CORRADO C, SU T, 1996. Skewness and kurtosis in SP 500 index returns implied by option prices[J]. Journal of financial research, 19: 175-192.

CORREDOR P, LECHO′ N P, SANTAMARı′A R, 2001. Option expiration effect in small markets: the Spanish stock exchange[J]. Journal of futures markets, 21: 905-928.

COUNTANT S, JONDEAU E, ROCKINGER M, 2001. Reading PIBOR futures options smiles: The 1997 snap election[J]. Journal of banking and finance, 25: 1957-1987.

COX J, ROSS S, 1976. The valuation of options for alternative stochastic processes[J]. Journal of financial economics, 3: 145-166.

CREMERS M, WEINBAUM D, 2010. Deviations from call-put parity and stock return predictability [J]. Journal of financial and quantitative analysis, 45: 335-367.

CRONQVIST H, FAHLENBRACH R, 2009. Large shareholders and corporate policies[J]. Review of financial studies, 22: 3941-3976.

CROUHY M, GALAI D, MARK R, 1998. Model risk [J]. Journal of financial engineering, 7: 267-288.

DANIEL K, GRINBLATT M, TITMAN S, WERMERS R, 1997. Measuring mutual fund performance with characteristic-based benchmarks[J]. The journal of finance, 52: 1035-1058.

DANIELSSON J, LOVE R, 2006. Feedback trading[J]. International journal of finance and economics, 11: 35-53.

DAOUK H, GUO J Q, 2004. Switching asymmetric GARCH and options on a volatility index[J]. Journal of futures markets, 24: 251-282.

DARRAT A, RACHMAN S, 1995. Has futures trading activity caused stock price volatility [J]. The journal of futures markets, 15: 537-557.

DAS S, SUNDARAM R, 1999. Of smiles and smirks: A term structure perspective[J]. Journal of financial and quantitative analysis, 34: 211-239.

DAY T E, 1993. Forecasting futures market volatility [J]. Journal of derivatives, 1: 33-50.

DAY T E, LEWIS C M, 1992. Stock market volatility and the information content of stock index options[J]. Journal of econometrics, 52: 267-287.

DE JONG F, DONDERS M, 1998. Intraday lead-lag relationships between the futures, options and Stock Markets[J]. European finance review, 337-359.

DEMODARAN A, LIM C, 1991. The effects of option trading on the underlying stocks' return processes [J]. Journal of banking and finance, 15: 647-664.

DENNIS P J, STRICKLAND D, 2002. Who blinks in volatile markets, individuals or institutions[J]. Journal of finance, 57: 1923-1949.

DERMAN E, KANI I, KAMAL M, 1997. Trading and hedging local volatility [J]. Journal of financial engineering, 6: 233-268.

DETEMPLE J, OSAKWE C, 2000. The valuation of volatility options [J]. European finance review, 4: 21-50.

DIAMOND D W, VERRECCHIA R E, 1987. Constraints on short-selling and asset price adjustment to private information [J]. Journal of financial economics, 18: 277-311.

DICKEY D A, FULLER W A, 1981. Likelihood ratio statistics for autoregressive time-series with a unit root[J]. Econometrica, 49: 1057-1072.

DIEBOLD F X, INOUE A, 2001. Long memory and regime switching [J]. Journal of econometrics, 105: 131-159.

DILTZ D, KIM S K, 1996. The relationship between stock and option price changes[J]. Financial review, 31: 499-519.

DING Z, GRANGER C W J, 1993. A long memory property of stock market returns and a new model[J]. Journal of empirical finance, 1(1): 83-106.

DOIDGE C, KAROLYI G A, STULZ R M, 2004. Why are foreign firms listed in the U.S. worth more[J]. Journal of financial economics, 71: 205-238.

DONALDSON R G, KAMSTRA M J, 2005. Volatility forecasts, trading volume, and the ARCH versus option-implied volatility trade off[J]. Journal of financial research, 28(4): 519-538.

DONDERS M, KOUWENBERG R, VORST T, 2000. Options and earnings announcements: An empirical study of volatility, trading volume, open interest, and liquidity[J]. European financial management, 6: 149-172.

DORAN J S, PETERSON D R, TARRANT B C, 2007. Is there information in the volatility Skew[J]. Journal of futures markets, 27: 921-959.

DOWNING C, ZHANG F, 2004. Trading activity and price volatility in the municipal bond market[J]. Journal of finance, 59: 899-931.

DRIESSEN J, MAENHOUT P, 2007. An empirical portfolio perspective on option pricing anomalies[J]. Review of finance, 11: 561-663.

DUFOUR A, ENGLE R F, 2000. Time and the price impact of a trade[J]. Journal of finance, 55: 2467-2498.

DUMAS B, FLEMING J, WHALEY R E, 1998. Implied volatility functions:

Empirical tests[J]. Journal of finance, 53: 2059-2106.

DUPIRE B, 1993. Model art[J]. Risk, 6: 118-121.

DVORˇÁK T, 2005. Do domestic investors have an information advantage? Evidence from Indonesia[J]. Journal of finance, 60: 817-839.

EASLEY D, KIEFER N, O'HARA M, 1997. The information content of the trading process[J]. Journal of empirical finance, 4: 159-186.

EASLEY D, O'HARA M, 1987. Price, trade size, and information in securities markets[J]. Journal of financial economics, 19: 69-90.

EASLEY D, O'HARA M, SRINIVAS P S, 1998. Option volume and stock prices: evidence on where informed traders trade[J]. Journal of finance, 53: 431-465.

EDELEN R, WARNER J, 2001. Aggregate price effects of institutional trading: a study of mutual fund flow and market returns[J]. Journal of financial economics, 59: 195-220.

EDERINGTON L, GUAN W, 2002. Is implied volatility an informationally efficient and effective predictor of future volatility[J]. Journal of risk, 4: 29-46.

EDERINGTON L, GUAN W, 2005. The information frown in option prices [J]. Journal of banking & finance, 29: 1429-1457.

EDERINGTON L, LEE J, 1993. How markets process information: News releases and volatility[J]. Journal of finance, 48: 1161-1191.

EDERINGTON L, LEE J H, 1996. The creation and resolution of market uncertainty: The impact of information releases on implied volatility[J]. Journal of financial and quantitative analysis, 31: 513-539.

Engle R F, 1982. Autoregressive conditional heteroscedasticity with estimates of the variance of United Kingdom inflation[J]. Econometrica, 50: 987-1007.

ENGLE R F, GRANGER C, 1987. Co-integration and error-correction: representation, estimation, and testing[J]. Econometrica, 55: 251-276.

ENGLE R F, NG V K, 1993. Measuring and testing the impact of news on volatility[J]. Journal of finance, 48: 1749-1778.

ERENBURG G, KUROV A, LASSER D J, 2006. Trading around macroeconomic announcements: Are all traders created equal[J]. Journal of financial intermediation, 15: 470-493.

EVANS M, LYONS R, 2002. Order flow and exchange rates dynamics[J]. Journal of political economy, 110: 170-180.

EVANS, M., LYONS, R., 2008. How is macro news transmitted to exchange rates[J]. Journal of Financial Economics 88, 26-50.

FAIR R C, SHILLER R J, 1990. Comparing information in forecasts from econometric models[J]. American economic review, 80: 375-389.

FAMA E F, MACBETH J D. Risk, return and equilibrium: Empirical tests [J]. Journal of political economy, 81: 607-636.

FAMA G, FRENCH K, 1992. The cross-section of expected stock returns [J]. Journal of finance, 47: 427-465.

FERREIRA M A, MATOS P, 2008. The colors of investors' money: the role of institutional investors around the world [J]. Journal of financial economics, 88: 499-533.

FIGLEWSKI S, 1981. The information effects of restrictions of short sales: Some empirical evidence[J]. Journal of financial and quantitative analysis, 16: 463-476

FIGLEWSKI S, 1989. Option arbitrage in imperfect markets[J]. Journal of finance, 44: 1289-1311.

FIGLEWSKI S, WEBB G P, 1993. Options, short sales, and market completeness[J]. Journal of finance, 48: 761-777.

FINUCANE T J, 1991. Put-call parity and expected returns[J]. Journal of financial and quantitative analysis, 26: 445-458.

FINUCANE T J, 1999. A new measure of the direction and timing of information flow between markets [J]. Journal of financial markets, 22: 135-151.

FLANNERY M, PROTOPAPADAGIS A, 2002. Macroeconomic factors do influence aggregate stock returns [J]. Review of financial studies, 15: 751-782.

FLEMING J, 1998. The quality of market volatility forecasts implied by s & p 100 index option prices[J]. Journal of empirical finance, 5: 317-345.

FLEMING J, OSTDIEK B, WHALEY R E, 1995. Predicting stock market volatility: A new measure[J]. Journal of futures markets, 15: 265-302.

FLEMING J, OSTDIEK B, WHALEY R E, 1996. Trading costs and the relative rates of price discovery in the stock, futures, and option markets [J]. Journal of futures markets, 16: 353-387.

FORNARI F, MELE A, 2001. Volatility smiles and the information content of news[J]. Applied financial economics, 11: 179-186.

FOSTER D, GALLAGHER D, LOOI A, 2011. Institutional trading and share returns[J]. Journal of banking and finance, 35: 3383-3399.

FOUCAULT T, 1999. Order flow composition and trading cost in a dynamic limit order book[J]. Journal of financial market 2, 99-134.

FRANKE G, STAPLETON R, SUBRAHMANYAM M, 1998. Who buys and

who sells options: The role of options in an economy with background risk [J]. Journal of economic theory, 82: 89-109.

FROOT K A, O'CONNELL P G J, SEASHOLES M S, 2001. The portfolio flows of international investors[J]. Journal of financial economics, 59: 151-193

FROOT K, RAMADORAI T, 2008. Institutional portfolio flows and international investments[J]. Review of financial studies, 21: 937-971.

GABAIX X, GOPIKRISHNAN P, PLEROU V, STANLEY H E, 2006. Institutional investors and stock market volatility[J]. Quarterly journal of economics, 121: 461-504.

GALAI D, 1983. The components of the return from hedging options against stocks[J]. Journal of business, 56: 45-54.

GARBADE K D, SILBER W L, 1982. Price movement and price discovery in the futures and cash markets[J]. Review of economics and statistics, 64: 289-297.

GARLEANU N, PEDERSEN L H, POTESHMAN A M, 2009. Demand-based option pricing[J]. Review of financial studies, 22: 4259-4299.

GEWEKE J, HUDAK S P, 1983. The estimation and application of long memory time series[J]. Journal of time series analysis, 4: 221-238.

GHOSH A, 1993. Cointegration and error correction models: Intertemporal causality between index and futures prices[J]. Journal of futures markets, 13: 193-198.

GLOSTEN L R, JAGANNATHAN R, RUNKLE D E, 1993. The relationship between expected value and the volatility of the nominal excess return on stocks[J]. Journal of finance, 48: 1779-1801.

GLOSTEN L R, MILGROM P R, 1985. Bid, ask and transaction prices in a specialist market with heterogeneously informed traders[J]. Journal of financial economics, 14: 71-100.

GLOSTEN L, 1994. Is the electronic open limit order book inevitable[J]. Journal of finance, 49: 1127-1161.

GOETTLER R L, PARLOUR C A, RAJAN U, 2005. Equilibrium in a dynamic limit order market[J]. Journal of finance, 60: 2149-2192.

GOETTLER R L, PARLOUR C A, RAJAN U, 2009. Informed traders and limit order markets[J]. Journal of financial economics, 93: 67-87.

GONÃCALVES S L, GUIDOLIN M, 2006. Predictable dynamics in the S&P 500 index options implied volatility surface[J]. Journal of business, 79(3): 1591-1635.

GOSPODINOV N, GAVALA A, 2006. Forecasting volatility[J]. Journal of forecasting, 25(6): 381-400.

GRAHAM M, NIKKINEN J, SAHLSTRöM P, 2003. Relative importance of scheduled macroeconomic news for stock market investors[J]. Journal of economics and finance, 27: 153-165.

GRANGER C W J, 1996. Investigating causal relations by econometric models and cross-spectral models[J]. Econometrica, 37: 424-438.

GRANGER C, NEWBOLD P, 1974. Spurious regression in econometrics[J]. Journal of econometrics, 2: 111-120.

GREEN C, 2004. Economic news and the impact of trading on bond prices [J]. Journal of finance, 59: 1201-1234.

GREEN T C, FIGLEWSKI S, 1999. Market risk and model risk for a financial institution writing options[J]. Journal of finance, 54: 1465-1499.

GRIFFIN J M, NARDARI F, STULZ R M, 2004. Are daily cross-border equity flows pushed or pulled[J]. Review of economics and statistics, 86 (3): 641-657.

GRIFFIN J, HARRIS J, TOPALOGLU S, 2003. The dynamics of institutional and individual trading[J]. Journal of finance, 58: 2285-2320.

GRINBLATT M, KELOHARJU M, 2000. The investment behavior and

performance of various investor types: A study of Finland's unique data set [J]. Journal of financial economics, 55: 43-67.

GRINBLATT M, TITMAN S, WERMERS R, 1995. Momentum investment strategies, portfolio performance and herding: a study of mutual fund behavior[J]. American economic review, 85: 1088-1105.

GROSSMAN S, 1988. An analysis of the implications for stock and future price volatility of program trading and dynamic hedging strategies [J]. Journal of business, 61: 275-298.

GROSSMAN S J, 1977. The existence of futures markets, noisy rational expectations and information externalities[J]. Review of economic studies, 44: 431-449.

GROSSMAN S J, 1997. A characterization of the optimality of equilibrium in incomplete markets[J]. Journal of economic theory, 15: 1-15.

GROSSMAN S J, MILLER M H, 1988. Liquidity and market structure[J]. Journal of finance, 43: 617-633.

GRÜNBICHLER A, LONGSTAFF F, 1996. Valuing futures and options on volatility[J]. Journal of banking and finance, 20: 985-1001.

GRUNBLICHER A, LONGSTAFF F, SCHWARTZ E, 1994. Electronic screen trading and the transmission of information: An empirical examination[J]. Journal of financial intermediation, 3: 166-187.

GUNTHER C B, 2004. Volatility trading in options market: How does it affect where informed traders trade[J]. Working paper,1-20

GUO D, 1998. The risk premium of volatility implicit in currency options[J]. Journal of business and economic statistics, 16: 498-507.

GUO D, 2000. Dynamic volatility trading strategies in the currency option market[J]. Review of derivatives research, 4(2): 133-154.

GUPTA N, YUAN K, 2009. On the growth effect of stock market liberalizations[J]. Review of financial studies, 22: 4715-4752.

GWILYM O A, BUCKLE M, 1999. Volatility forecasting in the framework of the option expiry cycle[J]. European journal of finance, 5: 73-94.

HANDA P, SCHWARTZ R, 1996. Limit order trading[J]. Journal of finance, 51: 1835-1861.

HANSEN L P, 1982. Large sample properties of generalized method of moments estimators[J]. Econometrica, 50: 1029-1054.

HARVEY C R, WHALEY R E, 1991. S&P 100 index option volatility[J]. Journal of finance, 46(4): 1151-1561.

HARVEY C R, WHALEY R E, 1992. Market volatility prediction and the efficiency of the S&P 100 Index option market[J]. Journal of financial economics, 31: 43-73.

HASBROUCK J, 1991. Measuring information content of stock trades[J]. Journal of finance, 46: 179-207.

HASBROUCK J, 1995. One security, many markets: Determining the contributions to price discovery[J]. The journal of finance, 50: 1175-1199.

HASBROUCK J, SEPPI D, 2001. Common factors in prices, order flows and liquidity[J]. Journal of financial economics, 59: 383-411.

HAU H, 2001. Location matters: An examination of trading profits[J]. Journal of finance, 56: 1951-1983.

Hee J A, Jangkoo K, Doojin R, 2008. Informed trading in the index option market: The case of KOSPI 200 options[J]. Journal of futures markets, 28(12): 1118-1146.

HEIMSTRA C, JONES J, 1994. Testing for linear and nonlinear Granger causality in the stock price-volume relation[J]. Journal of finance, 49: 1639-1664.

HENDERSON V, HOBSON D, HOWISON S, KLUGE T, 2003. A comparison of option prices under different pricing measures in a stochastic volatility model with correlation (working paper). Princeton, NJ:

Princeton University.

HENKER J, HENKER T, 2010. Are retail investors the culprits? Evidence from Australian individual stock price bubbles[J]. European journal of finance, 16: 281- 304.

HESTON S, 1993. A closed-form solution for options with stochastic volatility with applications to bond and currency options[J]. Review of financial studies, 6: 327-343.

HEUSON A, SU T, 2003. Intra-day behaviour of treasury sector index option implied volatilities around macroeconomic announcements[J]. Financial review, 38: 161-177.

HODRICK R J, PRESCOTT E C, 1997. Postwar U.S. business cycles: An empirical investigation[J]. Journal of money, credit banking, 29(1): 1-16.

HOLTHAUSEN R W, LEFTWICH R W, MAYERS D, 1987. The effect of large block transactions on security prices [J]. Journal of financial economics, 19: 237-267.

HONG H, STEIN J C, 1999. A unifed theory of underreaction, momentum trading, and short-term trading[J]. Journal of accounting and economics, 17: 69-94.

HONG H, STEIN J, 1999. A unified theory of under-reaction, momentum trading and overreaction in asset markets[J]. Journal of finance, 54: 2143-2184.

HONG H, STEIN J C, 2003. Differences of opinion, short-sales constraints, and market crashes[J]. The review of financial studies, 16: 487-525.

HSIEH D A, 1991. Chaos and nonlinear dynamics: application to Financial markets[J]. Journal of finance, 46: 1839-1877.

HUANG R D, STOLL H R, 1997. The components of the bid-ask spread: A general approach[J]. Review of financial studies, 10: 995-1034.

HULL J C, SUO W, 2002. A methodology for assessing model risk and its applications to the implied volatility function model[J]. Journal of financial and quantitative analysis, 37: 297-318.

HULL J C, WHITE A, 1987. Hedging the risks from writing foreign currency options[J]. Journal of international money and finance, 6: 131-152.

HULL J C, WHITE A, 1988. An analysis of the bias in option pricing caused by stochastic volatility[J]. Advances in futures and options research, 3: 29-61.

HVIDKJAER S, 2008. Small trades and the cross-section of stock returns [J]. Review of financial studies, 21: 1123-1151.

INDJEJIKIAN R J, 1991. The impact of costly information interpretation on firm disclosure decisions[J]. Journal of accounting research, 29: 277-301.

IORI G, 2002. A micro simulation of traders activity in the stock market: The role of heterogeneity, agents interactions and trade frictions[J]. Journal of economic behavior and organization, 49(2): 269-285.

JANK S, 2012. Mutual fund flows, expected returns, and the real economy. Journal of banking and finance, 36: 3060-3070.

JARROW R, RUDD A, 1982. Approximate option valuation for arbitrary stochastic processes[J]. Journal of financial economics, 10: 347-369.

JIANG G, TIAN Y, 2005. The model —free implied volatility and its information Content[J]. Review of financial studies, 18: 1305-1342.

JINJARAK Y, WONGSWAN J, ZHENG H, 2011. International fund investment and local market returns[J]. Journal of banking and finance, 35: 572-587.

JOHANSEN S, 1991. Estimation and hypothesis testing for cointegrating vectors in Gaussian vector autoregressive models[J]. Econometrica, 59: 1551-1580.

JOHANSEN S, 1992. Determination of cointegration rank in the presence of a linear trend[J]. Oxford bulletin of economics and statistics, 54: 383-397.

JOHN K, KOTICHA A, SUBRAHMANYAM M, 1991. The microstructure of options markets: Informed trading, liquidity, volatility and efficiency[J]. Working Paper, New York University.

JONDEAU E, ROCKINGER M, 2000. Reading the smile: The message conveyed by methods which infer risk neutral densities[J]. Journal of international money and finance, 19: 885-915.

JONES B, LIN C T, MASIH A, MANSUR M, 2005. Macroeconomic announcements, volatility, and interrelationships: An examination of the UK interest rate and equity markets[J]. International review of financial analysis, 14: 356-375.

JORION P, 1995. Predicting volatility in the foreign exchange market[J]. Journal of finance, 50: 507-528.

KALEV P, NGUYEN A, OH N, 2008. Foreign versus local investors: Who knows more? Who makes more[J]. Journal of banking and finance, 32: 2376-2389.

KAMESAKA A, NOFSINGER J R, KAWAKITA H, 2003. Investment patterns and performance of investor groups in Japan[J]. Pacific-basin finance journal, 11: 1-22.

KANG J, PARK H, 2008. The information content of net buying pressure:

Evidence from the KOSPI 200 index option market[J]. Journal of financial market, 11: 36-56.

KANG J K, PARK H J, 2006. The informed trades among three investor groups across three parallel markets - Evidence from Korea[J]. Working paper, 1-9.

KANG J, RYU D, 2010. Which trades move asset prices? An analysis of futures trading data[J]. Emerging markets finance and trade, 46 (1): 6-21.

KANG J, STULZ R M, 1997. Why is there a home bias? An analysis of foreign portfolio equity ownership in Japan [J]. Journal of financial economics, 46: 3-28.

KANIEL R, LIU H, 2006. So what orders do informed traders use[J]. Journal of business, 79: 1867-1913.

KANIEL R, SAAR G, TITMAN S, 2008. Individual investor trading and stock returns[J]. Journal of finance, 63: 273-310.

KAROLYI GA, 2002. Did the Asian financial crisis scare foreign investors out of Japan[J]. Pacific-Basin finance journal, 10: 411-442.

KEIM D B, MADHAVAN A, 1995. Anatomy of the trading process: empirical evidence on the behavior of institutional traders[J]. Journal of financial economics, 37: 371-398.

KELLEY E, WOIDTKE T, 2006. Investor protection and real investment by U.S. multinationals[J]. Journal of financial and quantitative analysis, 41: 541-572.

KIM E H, SINGAL V, 2000. Stock market openings: experience of emerging economies[J]. Journal of business, 73: 25-66.

KIM I J, KIM S, 2000. Price discovery role of the stock index futures and the stock index: a cointegration approach[J]. Korean journal of futures and options, 7: 87-115.

KIM I J, KIM S, 2004. Empirical comparison of alternative stochastic volatility option pricing models: evidence from Korean KOSPI 200 index options market[J]. Pacific-basin finance journal, 12: 117-142.

KIM I J, KIM S, 2005. Is it important to consider the jump component for pricing and hedging short-term options[J]. Journal of futures markets, 25: 989-1009.

KIM J, LANDI J, YOO S, 2009. Inter-temporal examination of trading activities of foreign investors in the Korean stock market[J]. Pacific-Basin finance journal, 17: 243-256.

KIM M, 2003. Implied volatility dynamics in the foreign exchange markets

[J]. Journal of international money and finance, 22: 511-528.

KIM O, VERRECCHIA R, 1991. Market reaction to anticipated announcements[J]. Journal of financial economics, 30: 273-309.

KIM O, VERRECCHIA R, 1991a. Trading volume and price reactions to public announcements[J]. Journal of accounting research, 29: 302-321.

KIM O, VERRECCHIA R, 1991b. Market reaction to anticipated announcements[J]. Journal of financial economics, 30: 273-310.

KIM O, VERRECCHIA R, 1994. Market liquidity and volume around earnings announcements [J]. Journal of accounting and economics, 17: 41-67.

KLEMKOSKY R, 1977. The impact and efficiency of institutional net trading imbalances[J]. Journal of finance, 32: 79-86.

KIM O, VERRECCHIA R E, 1997. Pre-announcement and event-period private information[J]. Journal of accounting and economics, 24: 395-420.

KOCH P D, 1993. Reexamining intraday simultaneity in stock index futures markets[J]. Journal of banking and finance, 17: 1191-1205.

KONSTANTINIDI E, SKIADOPOULOS G, 2008. Can the evolution of implied volatility be forecasted? Evidence from European and US implied volatility indices[J]. Journal of banking and finance, 32(11): 2401-2411.

KRAUS A, STOLL H R, 1972. Price impacts of block trading on the New York Stock Exchange[J]. Journal of finance, 27: 569-588.

KUMAR R, SARIN A, SHASTRI K, 1998. The impact of options trading on the market quality on the underlying security: An empirical analysis[J]. Journal of finance, 53: 717-732.

KYLE A S, 1985. Continuous auctions and insider trading[J]. Econometrica, 53: 1315-1336.

KYRIACOU K, SARNO L, 1999. The temporal relationship between derivatives trading and spot market volatility in the U. K.: Empirical analysis and monte carlo evidence[J]. The journal of futures markets, 19: 245-270.

LAKONISHOK J, LEE I, PEARSON N D, POTESHMAN A M, 2007. Option market activity[J]. Review of financial studies, 20: 813-857.

LAKONISHOK J, SHLEIFER A, VISHNY R W, 1992. The impact of institutional trading on stock prices[J]. Journal of financial economics, 32: 23-43.

LAMOUREUX C G, LASTRAPES W D, 1990a. Heteroskedasticity in stock return data: Volume versus GARCH effects [J]. Journal of finance, 45 (1): 221-229.

LAMOUREUX C G, LASTRAPES W D, 1990b. Persistence in variance, structural change and the GARCH model [J]. Journal of business and economic statistics, 8: 225-234.

LAMOUREUX C G, LASTRAPES W D, 1993. Forecasting stock return variance: Toward an understanding of stochastic implied volatilities [J]. The review of financial studies, 6: 293-326.

LATANE H A, RENDLEMAN R J, 1976. Standard deviations of stock price ratios implied in option prices[J]. Journal of finance, 31: 369-381.

LEE C M C, READY M J, 1991. Inferring trade direction from intraday data [J]. Journal of finance, 46: 733-746.

LEE J, YI C H, 2001. Trade size and information-motivated trading in the options and stock takeover[J]. Journal of business, 78: 1073-1098.

LEE Y, LIN J, LIU Y, 1999. Trading patterns of big versus small players in an emerging market: an empirical analysis [J]. Journal of banking and finance, 23: 701-725.

LEE Y, LIU Y, ROLL R, SUBRAHMANYAM, A., 2004. Order imbalances and market efficiency: evidence from the taiwan stock exchange [J].

Journal of financial and quantitative analysis, 39: 327-342.

LELAND H E, 1999. Beyond mean-variance: Performance measurement in a nonsymmetrical world[J]. Financial analysts journal, 55(1): 27-36.

LEUZ C, LINS KV, WARNOCK F E, 2009. Do foreigners invest less in poorly governed firms[J]. Review of financial studies, 22: 3245-3285.

LI W, WANG S, 2010. Daily institutional trades and stock price volatility in a retail investor dominated emerging market [J]. Journal of financial markets, 13: 448-474.

LIN J, SANGER G, BOOTH G, 1995. Trade size and components of the bid-ask spread[J]. Review of financial studies, 8: 1153-1183.

LIN M C, 2011. Information content for investor groups in TAIEX futures trading[J]. Asia-pacific journal of financial studies, 40: 433-466.

LIN W H, 2011. Does the put-call ratio forecast market returns? Evidence from an emerging market[J]. International research journal of finance and economics, 69: 95-107.

LIU J, LONGSTAFF F A, 2004. Losing money on arbitrage: Optimal dynamic portfolio choice in markets with arbitrage opportunities [J]. Review of financial studies, 17: 611-641.

LJUNG G M, BOX G E P, 1978. On a measure of lack of fit in time series models[J]. Biometrika,65: 297-303.

LLORENCE G, MICHAELY R, SAAR G, WANG J, 2002. Dynamic volume -return relation of individual stocks[J]. Review of financial studies, 15: 1005-1048.

LOVE R, PAYNE R, 2008. Macroeconomic news, order flows and exchange rates[J]. Journal of financial and quantitative analysis, 43: 467-488.

LOW C, 2004. The fear and exuberance from implied volatility of S&P 100 index options[J]. The journal of business, 77: 527-546.

MADHAVAN A, RICHARDSON M, ROOMANS M, 1997. Why do security prices change? [J]. A transaction-level analysis of NYSE stocks review of financial studies, 10: 1035-1064.

MANASTER S, RENDLEMAN R J, 1982. Option prices as predictors of equilibrium stock prices[J]. Journal of finance, 37: 1043-1057.

MAYHEW S, 1995. Implied volatility[J]. Financial Analyst Journal, 51: 8-20.

MAYHEW S, SARIN A, SHASTRI K, 1995. The allocation of informed trading across related markets: an analysis of the impact of changes in equity-option margin requirements[J]. Journal of finance, 1: 1635-1653.

MAYHEW S, STIVERS C, 2003. Stock return dynamics, option volume and the information content of implied volatility[J]. Journal of futures markets, 23(7): 615-646.

MCNICHOLS M, TRUEMAN B, 1994. Public disclosure, private information collection, and short - term trading [J]. Journal of accounting and economics, 17: 69-94.

MCQUEEN G, ROLEY V, 1993. Stock prices, news and business conditions [J]. Review of financial studies, 6: 683-707.

MELICK W, THOMAS C, 1997. Recovering an asset´s implied PDF from option prices: An application to crude oil during the Gulf Crisis [J]. Journal of financial and quantitative analysis, 32: 91-115.

MENDENHALL R R, 2004. Arbitrage risk and post-earnings-announcement drift[J]. Journal of business, 77: 875-894.

MENKHOFF L, OSLER C L, SCHMELING M, 2010. Limit - order submission strategies under asymmetric information[J]. Journal of banking and finance, 34: 2665-2677.

MERTON R C, 1973. Rational theory of option pricing[J]. Bell journal of economics and management science, 4: 141-183.

MERVILLE L J, PIEPTEA D R, 1989. Stock price volatility, mean-reverting diffusion, and noise[J]. Journal of financial economics, 24: 193-214.

MILLER E M, 1977. Risk, uncertainty, and divergence of opinion [J]. Journal of finance, 32: 1151-1168.

MILTON H, RAVIV A, 1993. Differences of opinion make a horse race[J]. The review of financial studies, 6(3): 473-506.

MORAUX F, NAVATTE P, VILLA C, 1999. The predictive power of the French market volatility index: A multi horizons study [J]. European finance review, 2: 303-320.

NAKAMURA H, SHIRATSUKA S, 1999. Extracting market expectations from option prices: Case studies in Japanese option markets[J]. Monetary and economic studies, 17: 1-43.

NAM S O, OH S Y, KIM H K, KIM B C, 2006. An empirical analysis of the price discovery and the pricing bias in the KOSPI 200 stock index derivatives markets [J]. International review of financial analysis, 15: 398-414.

NANDI S, 1998. How important is the correlation between returns and volatility in a stochastic volatility model? Empirical evidence from pricing and hedging in the S&P 500 index options market[J]. Journal of banking and finance, 22: 589-610.

NELSON D B, 1991. Conditional heteroskedasticity in asset returns: A new approach[J]. Econometrica, 59: 347-370.

NEWEY W K, WEST K D, 1987. A simple, positive, semi-definite, heteroscedasticity and autocorrelation consistent covariance matrix [J]. Econometrica, 55: 703-708.

NG L, WU F, 2007. The trading behavior of institutions and individuals in Chinese equity markets[J]. Journal of banking and finance, 31: 2695-2710.

NI S X, PAN J, POTESHMAN A M, 2008. Volatility information trading in the option market[J].the journal of finance, 63(3): 1059-1091.

NIKKINEN J, 2003. Normality tests of option-implied risk neutral densities: Evidence from the small Finnish market [J]. International review of financial analysis, 12: 99-116.

NIKKINEN J, SAHLSTRöM P, 2004. Impact of the federal open market committee´s meetings and scheduled macroeconomic news on stock market uncertainty[J]. International review of financial analysis, 13: 1-12.

NOFSINGER J R, PRUCYK B, 2003. Option volume and volatility response to scheduled economic news releases[J]. Journal of futures markets, 23: 315-345.

NOFSINGER J R, SIAS R, 1999. Herding and feedback trading by institutional and individual investors[J]. Journal of finance, 54: 2263-2295.

O'CONNOR M, 1999. The cross-sectional relationship between trading costs and lead/lag effects in stock and option markets[J]. Financial review, 34: 95-118.

ODEAN T, 1998. Are investors reluctant to realize their losses[J]. Journal of finance, 53: 1775-1798.

OFEK E, RICHARDSON M, WHITELAW R F, 2004. Limited arbitrage and short sales restrictions: Evidence from the option markets[J]. Journal of financial economics, 74: 305-342.

OH N, PARWADA J, 2007. Relations between mutual fund flows and stock market returns in Korea[J]. Journal of international financial markets, institutions and money, 17: 140-151.

OH N, PARWADA J, WALTER T, 2008. Investors' trading behavior and performance: online versus non-online equity trading in Korea[J]. Pacific-Basin finance journal, 16: 26-43.

OH S, HAHN S, 2008. Analyzing the cumulative returns on investments of domestic and foreign investors in Korean stock market[J]. Asia-pacific journal of financial studies, 37: 537-567.

OHANISSIAN A, RUSSEL J R, TSAY R S, 2008. True or spurious long memory? A new test[J]. Journal of business and economics statistics, 26(2): 161-175.

PAGAN A, 1984. Econometric issues in the analysis of regressions with generated regressions[J]. International economic review, 25: 221-247.

PAN J, POTESHMAN A M, 2006. The information in option volume for future stock prices[J]. Review of financial studies, 19: 871-908.

PARK K, BAE K, CHO J, 2006. Analyses on performance by different types of investors in Korean stock market[J]. Asia-Pacific journal of financial studies, 35: 41-76.

PARLOUR C A, 1998. Price dynamics in limit order markets[J]. Review of financial studies, 11: 786-816.

PATELL J M, WOLFSON M A, 1979. Anticipated information releases reflected in call option prices[J]. Journal of accounting and economics, 1: 117-140.

PATELL J M, WOLFSON M A, 1981. The extant and expost price effects of quarterly earnings announcements reflection in option and stock prices[J]. Journal of accounting research, 19: 434-458.

PHILLIPS S M, SMITH C W, 1980. Trading costs for listed options: The implications for market efficiency[J]. Journal of financial economics, 8: 179-201.

PIZZI M A, ECONOMOPOULOS A J, O'NEILL H M, 1998. An examination of the relationship between stock index cash and futures markets: a cointegration approach[J]. Journal of futures markets, 18: 297-305.

POON S H, GRANGER C, 2003a. Forecasting volatility in financial markets: A review[J]. Journal of economic literature, 41(2): 478-539.

PSYCHOYIOS D, SKIADOPOULOS G, ALEXAKIS P, 2003. A review of stochastic volatility processes: Properties and implications[J]. Journal of risk finance, 4: 43-60.

PUTTONEN V, 1993. Short sales restrictions and the temporal relationship between the stock and index cash and derivatives markets[J]. Journal of futures markets, 13: 645-664.

RANALDO A, 2004. Order aggressiveness in limit order book markets[J]. Journal of financial markets, 7: 53-74.

RICHARDS A, 2005. Big fish in small ponds: the trading behavior and price impact of foreign investors in Asian emerging equity markets[J]. Journal of financial and quantitative analysis, 40: 1-27.

RIGOBON R, 2003. Identification through heteroskedasticity[J]. Review of economics and statistics, 85: 777-792.

RIORDAN R, STORKENMAIER A, WAGENER M, ZANG S, 2013. Public information arrival: Price discovery and liquidity in electronic limit order markets[J]. Journal of banking and finance, 37: 1148-1159.

ROGERS J L, SKINNER D J, BUSKIRK A V, 2009. Earnings guidance and market uncertainty[J]. Journal of accounting and economics, 48: 90-109.

ROSS S A, 1976. The arbitrage theory of capital asset pricing[J]. Journal of economic theory, 13: 341-360.

ROSU I, 2009. A dynamic model of the limit order book [J]. Review of financial studies, 22: 4601-4641.

RUBINSTEIN M, 1994. Implied binomial trees[J]. The journal of finance, 49: 771-818.

SAMARAKOON L, 2009. The relation between trades of domestic and foreign investors and stock returns in Sri Lanka [J]. Journal of international financial markets, institutions and money, 19: 850-861.

SARWAR G, 2004. The informational role of options trading volume in the S&P 500 futures options markets[J]. Applied financial economics, 14: 1197-1210.

SARWAR G, 2005. The informational role of options trading volume in equity index options markets[J]. Review of quantitative finance and accounting, 24: 159-176.

SAVICKAS R, WILSON A, 2003. On inferring the direction of option trades [J]. Journal of financial and quantitative analysis, 38: 881-902.

SCHLAG C, STOLL H, 2005. Price impacts of options volume[J]. Journal of financial markets, 8: 69-87.

SCOTT L O, 1987. Option pricing when the variance changes randomly: Theory, estimation, and an application [J]. Journal of financial and quantitative analysis, 22: 419-438.

SCOTT L O, 1991. Random-variance option pricing: Empirical tests of the model and delta - sigma hedging [J]. Advances in futures and options research, 5: 113-135.

SENTANA E, FIORENTINI G, 2001. Identification, estimation and testing of conditionally heteroskedastic factor models [J]. Journal of econometrics, 102: 143-164.

SEPPI D J, 1997. Liquidity provision with limit orders and a strategic specialist[J]. Review of financial studies, 10: 103-150.

SEUNGMOOK C, WOHAR M E, 1992. The performance of the GPH estimator of the fractional difference parameter: Simulation results [J].

Review of quantitative finance & accounting, 2(4): 409-417.

SHEFRIN H, STATMAN M, 1985. The disposition to sell winners too early and ride losers too long: Theory and evidence[J]. Journal of finance, 40: 777-792.

SHEIKH A M, 1993. The behavior of volatility expectations and their effects on expected returns[J]. Journal of business, 66: 93-116.

SHIMKO D, 1993. Bounds of probability[J]. Risk, 6: 33-37.

SHLEIFER A, VISHNY R W, 1997. The limits of arbitrage[J]. The journal of finance, 52: 35-55.

SHYY G, VIJAYRAGHAVAN V, QUINN B.S, 1996. A further investigation of the lead-lag relationship between the cash market and the stock index futures market with the use of bidrask quotes: The case of France[J]. Journal of futures markets, 16: 240-405.

SIAS R, 2004. Institutional herding[J]. Review of financial studies, 17: 165-256.

SIAS R, STARKS L, 1997. Return autocorrelation and institutional investors [J]. Journal of financial economics, 46: 103-131.

SIAS R, STARKS L, TITMAN S, 2006. Changes in institutional ownership and stock returns: assessment and methodology[J]. Journal of business,

79: 2869-2910.

SIMON D P, 2003. The NASDAQ volatility index during and after the bubble [J]. Journal of derivatives, 11: 9-24.

SIMON D P, WIGGINGS R A, 2001. S&P futures and contrary sentiment indicators[J]. Journal of futures markets, 21: 447-462.

SKINNER J D, 1990. Option markets and the information content of accounting earnings releases[J]. Journal of accounting and economics, 13: 191-211.

SKINNER J D, 1997. Do option markets improve informational efficiency[J]. Contemporary accounting research, 14: 193-201.

SOPHIE X N, PAN J, POTESHMAN A M, 2008. Volatility information trading in the option market[J]. The journal of finance, 63: 1059-1091.

STEELEY J, 2001. A note on information seasonality and the disappearance of the weekend effect in the U.K. stock market[J]. Journal of banking and finance, 25: 1941-1956.

STEPHAN J A, WHALEY R E, 1990. Intraday price change and trading volume relations in the stock and option market[J]. Journal of finance, 45: 191-220.

STOLL H R, WHALEY R E, 1990. The dynamics of stock index and stock index futures returns[J]. Journal of financial and quantitative analysis, 25: 441-468.

STULZ R M, 2004. Should we fear derivatives [J]. Journal of economic perspectives, 18: 173-192.

TAUCHEN G, PITTS M, 1983. The price variability-volume relationship on speculative markets[J]. Econometrica, 51: 485-505.

TURKINGTON J, WALSH D M, 1999. Price discovery and casualty in the Australian share price index future markets [J]. Australian journal of management, 24 (2): 97-113.

VäHäMAA S, WATSKA S, ÄIJö J, 2005. What moves option-implied bond market expectations[J]. Journal of futures markets, 25: 817-843.

VARSON P L, SELBY M J P, 1997. Option prices as predictors of stock prices: Intraday adjustments to information releases [J]. The European journal of finance, 3: 49-72.

VEGA C, 2006. Stock price reaction to public and private information[J]. Journal of financial economics, 82: 103-133.

VERMA R, VERMA P, 2007. Noise trading and stock market volatility[J]. Journal of multinational financial management, 17: 231-243.

VERONESI P, 1999. Stock market reaction to bad news in good times: A rational expectation equilibrium model[J]. Review of financial studies, 12: 975-1007.

VERRECCHIA R E, 1981. On the relationship between volume reaction and consensus of investors: Implication for interpreting tests of information content[J]. Journal of accounting research, 19: 271-283.

VIJH A M, 1990. Liquidity of the CBOE equity options [J]. Journal of finance, 45(4): 1157-1179.

WAGNER N, MARSH T A, 2005. Surprise volume and heteroskedasticity in equity market returns[J]. Quantitative finance, 5(2): 153-168.

WAHAB M, LASHGARI M, 1993. Price dynamic and error correction in stock index and stock index futures: A cointegration approach[J]. Journal of futures markets, 13: 711-742.

WALSH D M, 1997. Price reaction to order flow 'news' in Australian equities[J]. Pacific basin finance journal, 5: 1-23.

WANG C, 2001. Investor sentiment and return predictability in agricultural futures markets[J]. Journal of futures markets, 21: 929-952.

WANG Y H, KESWANI A, TAYLOR S, 2006. The relationships between sentiment, returns and volatility [J]. International journal of forecasting, 22: 109-123.

WARTHER V A, 1995. Aggregate mutual fund flows and security returns[J]. Journal of financial economics, 39: 209-235.

WEBER E, 2010. Structural conditional correlation[J]. Journal of financial econometrics, 8: 392-407.

WEN L G H, CHIN S L, SHU F Y, 2008. Price discovery in the options markets: An application of put-call parity[J]. Journal of futures markets, 28(4): 354-375.

WERMERS R, 1999. Mutual fund herding and the impact on stock prices[J]. Journal of finance, 54: 581-601.

WEST K D, EDISON H J, CHO D, 1993. A utility-based comparison of some models of exchange rate volatility [J]. Journal of international economics, 35: 23-45.

WHALEY R E, 1982. Valuation of American call options on dividend-paying stocks[J]. Journal of financial economics, 10: 29-58.

WHALEY R E, 1993. Derivatives on market volatility: Hedging tools long overdue[J]. Journal of derivatives, 1: 71-84.

WHALEY R E, 2000. The investor fear gauge [J]. Journal of portfolio management, 26: 12-17.

WHALEY R, CHEUNG J, 1982. Anticipation of quarterly earnings announcements: A test of option market efficiency [J]. Journal of accounting and economics, 4: 57-83.

XING Y, ZHANG X, ZHAO R, 2010. What does individual option volatility smirk tell us about future equity returns [J]. Journal of financial & quantitative analysis, 45: 641-662

ZHAO Y, Wan D F, 2018. Institutional high frequency trading and price discovery: Evidence from an emerging commodity futures market [J]. Journal of futures markets, 38(2): 243-270.

강종만, 1993. 외국인투자가 증시에 미친 영향분석 [J]. 증권학회지, 9: 53-73.

고광수, 이준행, 2003, 외국인 거래 정보와 주식시장 개방 10 년의 경험 [J]. 재무연구, 16(1): 159-191.

고봉찬, 1997, 주가와 거래량: 반비모수적 접근방법 [J]. 재무연구, 10(1): 1-35

공재식, 1997, 한국주식시장에서의 거래량 정보효과에 관한 연구 [J]. 재무연구, 10(1): 37-68

구본일, 2000. 한국주식시장에서의 주가변동성의 비대칭에 관한 연구 [J]. 재무연구, 13: 129-159.

권택호, 이해문, 2000, KOSPI200 선물과 옵션거래가 주식시장의 변동

성에 미친 영향에 대한 실증분석 [J]. 재무연구, 13(2):103-133
김민호, 김민철, 2004, KOSPI200 옵션의 거래량, 미결제약정수량, 그리고 현물 주식시장의 변동성 [J]. 금융연구, 18(1):111-141.
김서경, 고광수, 2000, 주가지수와 주가지수선물관계의 일중거래 자료 분석 [J]. 증권학회지.27:101-137.
김서경, 홍정훈, 2004, 내재주가지수를 이용한 옵션시장과 주식시장의 상하관계에 관한 실증연구 [J].증권학회지, 33: 95-122
김서경, 홍정훈, 2004, 주가지수옵션시장과 주식시장에서의 일중 거래량과 가격 변동의 상호작용에 관한 연구 [J]. 선물연구, 32: 704-724
김성훈, 차동세, 2003, 금리패리티에 의해 암시된 선도환율의 정보적 유의성 분석 [J]. 선물연구, 11: 1-23
김솔, 김동석, 2000, 주가지수선물과 주가지수의 가격발견기능에 관한 실증 연구 :공적분과 오차수정모형 [J]. 선물연구, 7: 87-115.
김찬웅, 문규현, 2001, 우리나라 주식, 선물, 옵션시장에서의 선도/지연 효과에 관한 연구 [J]. 재무관리연구, 18(1): 129-157.
문성주, 2004, KOSPI200 지수옵션 변동성의 정보내용 [J]. 산업경제연구, 17(6): 2474-2490
연강흠, 1994, 증시 개방 후의 투자 주체별 투자 행태에 관한 연구

[J]. 증권학회지, 16: 151~189

이인섭,고광수, 1994,한국증시에서 개인,기관,외국인투자가의 투자 행태 연구 [J]. 재무연구, 8: 45~74

원재환, 2005, 한국금융시장에서 파생상품 도입의 가격효과 [J].금융 연구 19(1):152-181.

박준용, 정규승, 2003, 한국과 미국 주식 시장의 동조화에 관한 연구 [J]. 한국 경제의 분석, 9(1):2-86.

박진우, 김민혁, 2003, 정보와 주가변동성 [J]. 증권학회지, 32(2): 141-160.

송치영, 2002, 뉴스가 금융시장에 미치는 영향에 관한 연구 [J]. 국제 경제연구, 8(3): 1-34.

선정훈, 정일준, 2002, 통화정책뉴스가 주가에 미치는 영향 [J]. 금융 경제연구, 140: 1-24.

옥기율, 장우애, 2008.주가변동성에 대한 KOSPI200 지수옵션의 투자 자별 거래량의 정보적 역활 [J]. 경영연구, 23(2):47-67.

옥기율, 1997.주가변동성의 비대칭적 반응에 관한 실증적 연구 [J]. 증권학회지, 21: 295-324

옥기율,허화, 천성진, 2006. KOSPI200 의 변동성 추정방법에 따른 VaR 비교 연구 [J]. 금융공학연구, 5(1): 21-39

이필상, 민준선(1997), "주가지수선물 수익율과 현물 수익율간의 일중 관계에 관한 연구 [J] .재무관리연구, 14: 141-169.

최병욱, 2011.옵션거래량 정보는 현물가격을 예측하는가?: KOSPI200 옵션시장에 대한 실증분석 [J] .한국증권학회지, 40(4):551-578